CreditBooster™:
Ultimate Guide to a Better Credit Score

CreditBooster™: Ultimate Guide to a Better Credit Score

Published by
InCharge® Education Foundation, Inc.
2101 Park Center Drive, Suite 310
Orlando, FL 32835
www.inchargefoundation.org

Cover design by Blue Studios, Inc.

ISBN-10: 0-9769398-5-1
ISBN-13: 978-0-9769398-5-6

InCharge® and the starburst logo are trademarks of InCharge® Institute of America, Inc.

Library of Congress Control Number: 2006923049

Printed in the United States of America

10 9 8 7 6 5 4 3 2 1

A Message from the InCharge® Education Foundation, Inc.

Thank you for choosing **CreditBooster**™.

At the InCharge® Education Foundation, we believe you're more likely to achieve "financial wellness" and success if you combine your knowledge, energy, and commitment in your daily financial transactions and decisions. We have developed **CreditBooster**™ to be a tool you can use to guide these activities.

Our writers and researchers have worked hard at combining the most up to date knowledge of the credit and credit scoring industries with success strategies that have the best chance of working for you if you choose to implement them.

Your credit report is a flexible document that changes regularly. With understanding of the process and proper action, you can feel more confident in managing your credit rating.

Best wishes to those of you who have taken on the challenge to manage their financial future in this positive, dedicated manner. And thank you for allowing InCharge® Education Foundation to be your guide on this rewarding journey.

Your credit reports and scores are extremely important pieces of your total personal financial puzzle. There are many other important areas of personal finance, such as debt reduction and proper credit management that also need your regular attention. We invite you to learn more about all of the resources that are available from InCharge® Education Foundation to help you stay "InCharge® of your finances for Life," by visiting us at www.inchargefoundation.org.

The Editors
InCharge® Education Foundation, Inc.

Table of Contents

Chapter	Page

Introduction

Have you noticed over the past few years that you've been hearing more and more about your credit reports and credit scores? The secret is finally out when it comes to credit scores; well, part of the secret is out. The part about how really important your credit reports and scores are to your financial future. Other parts of the secret are still largely under wraps and being leaked out very slowly.

For years, lenders and others in the financial services industries were content to keep the details of exactly how you and your fellow consumers were judged creditworthy or not, confined to the knowledge bank of credit industry insiders. In fact, even veteran loan officers and credit grantors were never exactly quite sure how the system of credit scoring actually worked.

This, keeping everyone in the dark, was, reportedly, by design. Fair Isaac and Company, the organization that developed the proprietary system of attaching a score to a consumer using input from credit reports, popularly known as the "FICO®" score, had a financial interest in protecting its product's design so that it could not be copied. Fair Isaac licenses its scoring system to Credit Bureaus who, in turn, sell credit score information to businesses and consumers. Keeping product design secrets is common in business, but few products affect all of us so personally. And, few other products offer the opportunity for information and scoring to be used to deny us financial opportunity, rightly or wrongly.

This system was firmly in place for dozens of years until 2003 when Congress had finally heard enough horror stories from consumers who were turned down for credit and loans without really knowing why they were turned down. More importantly, these consumers, perhaps you are one of them, had no idea of what they needed to do to improve their credit score in order to become more creditworthy in the future. Basically, we consumers did not know the rules of the game yet we are expected to play the game, and do everything correctly, or expect to be punished with a lower credit score and less financial opportunity.

Since you are reading this book you are obviously someone who wants to learn the rules of the credit game, so let us commend you. And, you've chosen a good time to become fluent in the language of the credit industry because it has never been more important for us to understand and manage our credit. Credit reports are truly each person's Financial Resume, and more and more important people are reviewing your report. It is reported that nearly half of employers routinely check credit reports when making hiring decisions. And this is not confined to people who only work with money. Employees in all job categories are having their credit checked when applying for a job and, perhaps, as a matter of routine during employment in many companies.

Plus, insurance companies, landlords, utility companies, retail stores, and many businesses now use credit reports and credit scores to judge you every day. In fact, if your credit score decreases by too many points in a short period of time, for some reason, perhaps you have been late on a few car payments, under the relatively new Universal Default penalty, now used by a growing number of creditors, all of your interest rates could suddenly increase by double digits.

Advances in technology are allowing easy and relatively inexpensive access to your credit information to be made widely available to a growing number of interested parties. Computer access to records with a just few clicks on a keyboard in a matter of seconds makes it an easier decision for businesses to use the credit report. And, electronic delivery of this information makes the cost just a fraction of what it used to be.

Cheap and fast information that is a valuable indicator of your ability to manage your finances as well as other aspects of your life, is simply too good to resist. And, technology is allowing more information to be compiled about you more quickly. There really is no way to escape one's financial missteps these days.

You can learn a great deal about a person based on how they manage their own finances and so your credit information is very valuable to anyone trying to make decisions about you. For these reasons you must ensure that whatever is reported on your credit reports is 100 percent accurate and up to date. It is your right to have accurate information and the process of keeping your credit reports updated can be tedious and difficult at times if you are not familiar with the procedures of the credit bureaus. **CreditBooster**™ is your roadmap to dealing with the credit bureaus and making sure your financial resume is a true reflection of your money management history. It is also your guide to making improvements so that you can get past any negative damage to your credit history and increase your credit worthiness.

CreditBooster™ is designed to lead you through a step-by-step process to enhance your usage of credit and management of your debt. Our goal is to get you INVOLVED in planning and working toward your financial health and "wellness." The format of **CreditBooster**™ should serve as a useful tool that you can use to realize these financial goals.

SECTION I: CREDIT AND YOU presents an overview of the purposes and characteristics of credit as a useful tool to help you realize given lifestyle goals.

Chapter 1: Basics of Improving Your Credit outlines the types of credit available, the uses of that credit, and the problems associated with using credit.

SECTION II: ASSESSING YOUR FINANCIAL STATUS helps you focus on some important components that affect your personal financial standing. It thus looks at the same basic financial information that lenders use to assess your credit status. The goal here is to provide you with a realistic picture of your financial status.

Chapter 2: Where Do You Stand? helps you identify and calculate your current net worth, a basic element of your financial health that is based on your assets and liabilities.

Chapter 3: Where Does All the Money Go? helps you determine the basics of your cash flow, in terms of your income and your expenses.

Chapter 4: Making Sense of Your Financial Situation helps you compute, using the information we've presented in Chapter 2 and Chapter 3, various financial ratios, which are calculations that help you assess your financial standing in relation to applying and obtaining credit.

SECTION III: ASSESSING YOUR DEBT STATUS outlines how your financial/credit status is assessed in standard measures that others can use to determine whether or not to extend you additional credit:

Chapter 5: Understanding Your Credit Report and Your Credit History explains how your credit history is recorded in a formal credit reporting system.

Chapter 6: Understanding Your Credit Score provides detail on the purpose of the credit score, which "measures" your credit history, how it is used by potential lenders, and how you can obtain those scores.

SECTION IV: THE FIX IS ON! helps you begin the real work of taking the right steps to improve your credit status. Here you will start taking the actions necessary to reduce your debt load and rebuild your credit.

Chapter 7: Setting Your Financial Goals helps you focus on setting financial goals that boost your credit status.

Chapter 8: Getting Your Financial House in Order helps you develop a spending plan that will help you reach the financial goals you formed in Chapter 7.

Chapter 9: Removing Mistakes from Your Credit Report provides you assistance and advice in spotlighting errors and omissions in your credit reports and correcting those mistakes.

Chapter 10: Improving Your Credit Score provides you assistance and advice in improving your credit score.

Chapter 11: Resolving Severe Credit Problems on Your Own leads you on a do-it-yourself approach to problems focusing on steps the debtor can take on his own to address severe credit difficulties such as multiple past due accounts, repossessions and accounts turned over to collection agencies the problems.

Chapter 12: Getting Help for Resolving Severe Debt Problems outlines steps you can take when you just can't fix things yourself, directing you to credit counseling and debt management plans that can partner with you in addressing your severe credit problems.

SECTION V: SPECIAL CASES addresses three specific situations that are particularly complex/difficult to resolve. The purpose here is just to identify factors that you may have to examine. Given the circumstances, these complex issues probably require you consulting with certified professionals who can give you appropriate guidance.

Chapter 13: Building Credit When You Do Not Have Any helps those who are credit "beginners"—they haven't built up any credit history—to begin building up a "status" that lenders can examine when making credit decisions.

Chapter 14: Building Credit after Divorce addresses the specific factors related to divorce and credit history/usage.

Chapter 15: Rebuilding Credit after Bankruptcy addresses those factors that are related to post-bankruptcy credit management.

The purpose of **CreditBooster**™ is to help you gain control—maybe mastery—over the factors that affect your credit rating, so you can be InCharge® of your credit score and boost your financial health. Each chapter has two main components to help you on this journey:

What You Need to Know!, which provides the information you need to make the right decisions and take the proper steps; and **What You Can Do!**, which, using the knowledge you gained from **What You Need to Know!**, leads you through the various steps and activities you can take to Boost Your Credit.

All worksheets used in this book can be downloaded for your use at our web site: www.creditbooster.com. Let's get started with *Section I*, addressing the basics of improving your credit.

| Chapter | **1** | | Basics of Improving Your Credit |

What You Need To Know!

It is clear that obtaining credit is easy today. You probably receive five or more credit offers in the mail each week. You can walk into any major retail chain store and open a charge account in minutes and begin borrowing. For many people, obtaining credit is too easy.

Why are retailers so willing to have you "charge it"? Studies show that consumers tend to spend approximately 20 percent more at retail stores when they use a credit card. For many people, such spending goes well beyond the income available to cover the bills when they come due. And even for those people who can afford the payment, the interest paid is a huge burden for borrowers and a huge income source for lenders.

Easy Access to Credit Can Create Problems for Many People

Credit can be a useful, and sometimes even necessary, tool. However, easy access to credit causes many consumers to spend more than they can afford. You may feel that your debts have become so burdensome that they negatively affect your relationships and your ability to care for your children, save for retirement and even sleep at night. As do many people, you may fear that unforeseen expenses—medical bills, layoffs, or major home or auto repairs—will result in unpaid debts or even bankruptcy.

> **In 2005, more than 2 million Americans declared bankruptcy as a result of runaway-debt problems.**

What can you do to establish good credit? What can you do to avoid credit problems? How can you rebuild your credit if you already have problems? This book is designed to give you the tools you will need. To begin, let's look at some basic aspects of credit.

What Is Credit?

Credit is simply the use of someone else's money with the understanding (and promise) that you will give it back in the future. In return, most lenders expect the borrower to pay interest while the money is owed. There are also various fees that lenders sometimes charge; usually when the loan is first granted.

Because of these fees, the percentage rate used to calculate the interest does not tell the whole story. Accordingly, the law requires that lenders tell you the **annual percentage rate (APR)** in advance of taking out a loan. The APR represents the true cost of credit and can be used to compare offers from various lenders. The APR is based on the **finance charge** that is the total dollar cost of all mandatory charges for the loan, not just the interest. The law requires that the lenders disclose the finance charge in advance if it can be calculated. An example might be a credit card where the finance charge depends on the amount owed on the card. In such cases, the finance charge need not be stated in advance.

Credit usually comes in two forms. **Installment credit** is a loan of money or the purchase of an item with the promised to repay the full amount plus any finance charges over a period of time in nearly equal payments (installments), usually monthly. An example of an installment loan is a loan to buy a new car. **Open-end credit** involves an agreement to loan money or purchase items at any time in the future as long as the total loan amount does not exceed some agreed-upon credit limit set by the lender. Credit cards are the most common example of open-end credit.

The Five C's of Credit

What does a lender look at to determine if you should be approved for a loan? While lenders make their own decisions based on their own criteria, the criteria they use fit into five categories known as the "Five C's" of credit. They are:

- **CAPACITY** refers to the ability to repay the loan. In other words, can the borrower afford the monthly payments based on his or her income?

- **CAPITAL** refers to the borrower's bank account balances, ownership of major assets, such as a house or car, and the overall level of debt being carried by the borrower.

- **CONDITIONS** refers to the state of the national economy and the availability of money to lend. Credit is harder to get in bad economic times.

- **COLLATERAL** is an asset pledged against a loan to give the lender more security that the loan will be repaid. The lender is more confident about getting at least some of the money back when there is collateral.

- **CHARACTER** is the lender's assessment of the borrower's prior success in repaying loans. Consumers who have failed to repay loans as agreed-to in the past will find that credit is harder to get and more expensive in the future.

Taken together the five C's of credit provide the lender with the information needed to make the decision to grant credit.

Appropriate Uses of Credit

Years ago, many people felt that being in debt was always bad and that people with debts, other than possibly a home mortgage, were not managing their money very well. Today, credit usage is very common. Many people owe money to ten or more lenders. Such people are likely to be having credit difficulties. Some of them may never be totally out of debt.

This is not to say that all credit usage is bad. Credit, when used wisely, can be very helpful to consumers. Indeed, recognition of these benefits is probably why you are so concerned about your own credit situation. So, when is credit usage appropriate? A short list of good uses of credit would include:

- **A MORTGAGE ON A HOME** – With a mortgage, you are buying an asset that will likely go up in value and the interest on the loan is tax deductible.

- **STUDENT LOANS TO PAY FOR DIRECT EDUCATION EXPENSES** – Student loans are an investment in the future that can pay off in several hundred thousands of dollars in extra income over one's working life.

- **BUSINESS LOANS TO START OR EXPAND A PROFITABLE BUSINESS** – Most new business start-ups require financing through loans. Successful businesses can support such borrowing.

- **MEDICAL EXPENSES** – Maintaining one's health fits just about everyone's definition of a "need." Letting a health problem go untreated due to lack of ready cash often leads to even more severe and expensive health problems later on.

Note that each of these items is one for which most people would have a hard time coming up with all the necessary cash. The key is to borrow as little as possible for these purposes by using savings whenever possible.

Why It Is So Easy to Develop Credit Problems

If using credit can be appropriate sometimes, why do so many people get into trouble with credit? There are two basic reasons. First, while the purpose for borrowing money might be appropriate, the amount borrowed may not be. Second, many people use credit for inappropriate reasons. They see a "needed" goal and credit seems to be an easy way to achieve it. That is what gets people get into trouble. They see achieving the goal before they see the trouble credit can bring.

Using credit postpones the need to pay. It solves an issue today—not having enough money for some purpose—by putting it off until tomorrow. As a result, credit can be very tempting—far more tempting than the recognition of the future obligations involved. Psychological studies have shown that people overestimate the discomfort of not being able to have something they "need" right away. And they underestimate the difficulty of paying the debt that comes from meeting that "need." You might say that people are overly optimistic—to their own detriment.

In some cases, loan interest can be greater than the original amount borrowed!

Taking Responsibility

It is easy to blame the banks and credit card companies for the debt problems that are so common today. Certainly, they could be more careful to whom they loan money. But they only make credit available. It is consumers who use it. Sometimes they do so because they have overspent their income. Sometimes they have had financial setbacks such as job loss or illness.

The reasons don't matter. Repaying a debt is the responsibility of the borrower. Solving the problem, whether it is the repayment itself or the bad credit reputation that comes with over-indebtedness, is also the borrower's responsibility.

Of course, you already know this. You may be having debt problems now for which you are eager to take responsibility. Or perhaps you just want to establish (or reestablish) a good credit reputation to show that you are a responsible consumer. Helping you achieve those two goals is the purpose of **CreditBooster**™. So let's get going.

Resolving Credit Problems

Like all problems, correcting credit problems takes action. If your problem is a poor or non-existent credit history, you would want to get a clear picture of your credit history that is on file with the major credit reporting agencies. If your problem is excess debt, you will want to stop using credit. That might mean cutting up your credit cards or, at minimum, leaving home without them. You have probably heard the phrase, "when you are in a hole—stop digging." You certainly would not want to take on additional debts, and you would want to reduce the ones you already owe.

As we outlined above, **CreditBooster**™ uses a two-phase process to help you address your credit usage. The first phase involves learning about credit so that your efforts can be based on knowledge. The second phase involves action. Accordingly, each chapter in **CreditBooster**™ has two main headings—**What You Need to Know!** and **What You Can Do!**—to reflect these two phases.

Getting out of debt means that you must face the situation head-on with a clear focus on the reality of the situation. Excessive debt may be destroying your life, dreams, and perhaps your career and family. You can—you will—be in charge of your finances, get out of debt, and stay out of debt. From now on getting out of debt is the top priority in your financial life.

> **Whether you start paying off debts with the smallest debt or the one with the highest interest rate, just start!!!**

What You Can Do!

Action Module 1A

Properly managing your debt and credit usage requires that you know exactly how much you owe, to whom, and at what cost. You will need to create a debt inventory for yourself. One key to success in getting a clear picture is setting a target date for getting each debt paid off. Installment loans have a date identified when the final payment will pay the debt in full, but credit cards do not. Take the time now to complete your debt inventory. *Action Module 1A: Example of a Debt Inventory* provides a sample debt inventory listing all the debts for an illustrative borrower, so you can see what data goes where. Then referencing Table 1, use *Action Module 1B: Your Debt Inventory* to identify your target dates.

Action Module 1A | Example of A Dept Inventory

Account	Limit or Original Amount Borrowed	APR	Balance	Payoff Date (in months)	Monthly Payment*	Comments
Consolidation Loan	$5000	9%	$4,690	77	$80.44	Low APR
Car Loan	$11,500	8%	$9,300.	38	$280 75	Loan originally for 48 months
Credit Card 1 (joint account)	$5,000	12%	$1,100	36	$36.53	Low APR, available balance
Credit Card 2	$3,000	14%	$500	36	$17.09	Low APR, available balance
Credit Card 3	$6,000	20%	$4,800	36	$178.37	High APR, high balance
Credit Card 4	$3,000	22%	$1,600	36	$61.10	High APR, low balance
TOTAL	$33,500		$21,990		$654 28	High payments, high interest

Because credit cards do not have a set payoff date, you will need to select a payoff date for all your credit cards

Action Module 1B | Your Debt Inventory

Account	Limit or Original Amount Borrowed	APR	Balance	Payoff Date (in months)	Monthly Payment*	Comments
TOTAL		N/A				

*Because credit cards do not have a set payoff date, you will need to select a payoff date for all your credit cards
This worksheet is available for download at www.creditbooster.com/downloads/.

You can use Table 1 to determine the monthly payment needed to pay off credit cards within the time period desired. This table presents monthly payments per $1000 of credit card debt. Let's say you owe $3,500 on a card with a 15% APR that you want to pay off in 30 months. Here's how you would calculate the monthly payment:

1. First locate the amount in the table that corresponds to a 15% APR for a payoff in 30 months. The amount is $40.18. This is the payment if your debt is $1000.

2. Divide the debt you want to pay off by $1000. In our example, $3,500 divided by $1,000 is 3.5.

3. Multiply the result from step 2 by the result from step 1. In our example, 3.5 times $40.18 equals $140.63. These payments will payoff the $3,500 owed in 30 months.

Table 1 | Number of Monthly Payments Till Payoff Date

APR	12	18	24	30	36	48	60
9	$87.45	$59.59	$45.68	$37.35	$31.80	$24.88	$20.76
10	87.92	60 06	46.14	37 81	32 27	25.36	21 25
11	88.38	60.52	46.61	38.28	32.74	25.85	21.74
12	88.85	60 98	47.07	38 75	33 21	26.33	22 24
13	89 32	61.45	47 54	39.22	33.69	26 83	22.75
14	89.79	61 92	48.01	39.70	34 18	27.33	23.27
15	90 26	62.38	48 49	40.18	34.67	27 83	23.79
16	90.73	62.86	48.96	40.66	35.16	28.34	24.32
18	91 68	63.81	49.92	41.64	36.15	29.37	25.39
20	92.63	64.76	50.90	42.63	37.16	30.43	26.49
22	93.59	65 73	51.88	43 63	38 19	31.51	27 62
24	94.56	66.70	52.87	44.65	39.23	32.60	28.77

For time periods and APRs other than for those in Table 1, visit the InCharge® website at www.mindyourfinances.org and then "more" at the Financial Tools Channel.

We will use the information in your credit inventory later in *Section II* of this book. The information will allow you to determine the degree of your debt problems by calculating certain ratios comparing your debt to your income and your debt to your assets. You will also determine your net worth (assets minus liabilities) and develop an income and expense statement to see how far you are coming out ahead or behind each month.

Action Module 1C

Action Module 1C asks you to identify the terms for all of your debts, including interest rate, late payment fees, grace periods, etc. Basically it tells you the terms and requirements of your accounts. You will use the information in *Action Module 1C: My Credit Account Rules* throughout **CreditBooster**™ to assess and fix any credit problems you might have.

Action Module 1C | My Credit Account Rules

Card Term or Requirement	Example: Town Bank Credit Card	Loan A	Credit Card B	Credit Card C
What is the Credit Limit?	$12,000			
What is the typical due date?				
What is the APR (for loan accounts)?	18 0%			
What is the APR for purchases (for credit cards)?	12.99%			
What is the APR for balance transfers (for credit cards)?	9.99%			
What is the APR for Cash Advances (for credit cards)?	17.99%			
What is the default rate (APR) on the account?	27.99% (see notes below)			
Is the APR rate variable or fixed?	Variable			
If the APR is variable, how is it calculated?	Prime plus 9% for purchases; prime plus 6% for transfers; prime plus 14% for cash advances; prime plus 24% for default rate			

(continued)

(continued)

Card Term or Requirement	Example: Town Bank Credit Card	Loan A	Credit Card B	Credit Card C
What is the grace period for repayment of credit card purchases?	20 days if you pay your new balance in full each billing period by the due date			
What is the grace period for credit card cash advances and balance transfers?	None			
How is the balance computed (for credit cards)?	Average Daily Balance (including new purchases)			
Is there an annual fee on the account? How much is it?	$35			
What is the minimum finance charge?	$1.00			
What is the transaction fee for credit card cash advances and balance transfers?	The higher of $20 or 3%			
What is the late payment fee on the account?	$25 on balances up to $500, $35 on balances over $500.			
What is the over the limit fee (for credit cards)?	$40			

Because credit cards do not have a set payoff date, you will need to select a payoff date for all your credit cards.

This worksheet is available for download at www.creditbooster com/downloads/.

Summary

- Credit is easy to get, and easy credit causes significant financial problems for millions of Americans. The average American household carries an average balance of more than $7,000 in credit card debt and pays more than $1,000 in interest annually.

- Credit is simply the use of someone else's money. The cost of credit is measured in dollars as a finance charge and as a percentage called the annual percentage rate (APR).

- The five C's of credit—capacity, capital, conditions, collateral, and character—refer to factors used by lenders when making decisions about whom to grant credit.

- There are some appropriate uses for credit, including home mortgages, student loans, and business loans. But avoid taking on any more debt than you can afford.

- It is easy to develop credit problems. These problems include the level of debt itself and the interest charges and other costs of borrowing.

- Responsible consumers know that it is their responsibility to pay debts and maintain a good credit history.

- The process of resolving credit problems begins with knowledge and ends with action. An important first assessment step is creating a debt inventory listing all debts owed, to whom, and under what conditions.

Section I: Credit and You presented an overview of the purposes and characteristics of credit as a useful tool to help you realize given lifestyle goals. Now let's move on now to *Section II: Assessing Your Financial Status*, where we help you focus on some important components that affect your personal financial standing.

Chapter 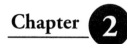 2 | Where Do You Stand?

In this chapter, we'll help you focus on some important components that reflect your personal financial standing.

What You Need To Know!

Before you can work on your credit status and improve your credit score, you need to determine your current financial situation. You need to know precisely where you stand. What do you own? What do you owe? Does what you own exceed what you owe? Or is it the other way around? This chapter addresses each of these questions and more. It will allow you to determine your current financial status.

Your current financial status is measured by the difference between what you own and what you owe:

- Your **assets** are the things you own.
- Your **liabilities** are what you owe.
- Your **net worth** is the difference between the two.

If you have been worrying about the state of your finances, you might be reassured by what you find in this chapter. Or you might find out that your fears are well-founded. You might even learn that things are worse than you thought. No matter. Simply knowing where you stand is a good thing. This is because worry does not solve problems. Action solves problems. And action begins with a clear understanding of reality.

What You Own!

It may seem simple enough to figure out what you own. But many people overlook things. In addition, they often put an improper value on their assets. An asset is worth the amount it would bring if you were to sell it. This amount is referred to as the item's **fair market value**. It is not what you paid for the asset nor its value after subtracting any debt owed on it (debts are subtracted later). Simply make your best estimate of what the asset would sell for if you were to sell it today.

Assets can be divided into three groups—monetary, use, and investment. The next three worksheets will help you list your assets and record their values.

Worksheet 2A: Monetary Assets

Monetary assets include cash, bank accounts and money market mutual funds. They are sometimes called cash equivalents because you can turn them into cash very easily.

Worksheet 2A | Monetary Assets

Monetary Assets	Fair Market Value
Cash on Hand	
Checking #1	
Checking #2	
Savings #1	
Savings #2	
Savings #3	
CD #1	
CD #2	
Money Market Fund #1	
Money Market Fund #2	
Other Monetary Assets	
TOTAL MONETARY ASSETS	

This worksheet is available for download at www.creditbooster.com/downloads/

Worksheet 2B: Use Assets

Use assets are items you own that help you get through your day-to-day life. Clothing, a home, furniture, appliances and a vehicle are all examples of use assets.

Worksheet 2B | Use Assets

Use Assets	Fair Market Value
Vehicle #1	
Vehicle #2	
Vehicle #3	
First Residence	
Second Residence	
Home Furnishings	
Clothing	
Jewelry	
Recreational Items	
Personal Property	
Other Vehicles	
Other Use Assets	
TOTAL USE ASSETS	

This worksheet is available for download at www.creditbooster.com/downloads/.

Worksheet 2C: Investment Assets

Investment assets are those that you own and hope to make money off of them either because they might go up in value or pay you some income such as rents from an apartment building you might own.

Worksheet 2C | Investment Assets

Investment Assets	Fair Market Value
Employer Ret. Acct. #1	
Employer Ret. Acct. #2	
IRA Account #1	
IRA Account #2	
Brokerage Account #1	
Brokerage Account #2	
Mutual Fund #1	
Mutual Fund #2	
Real Estate Investments	
Collectibles	
Other Investment Assets	
TOTAL INVESTMENT ASSETS	

This worksheet is available for download at www.creditbooster.com/downloads/

What You Owe!

Your liabilities include any debts you legally owe to others. People can owe money on their homes, vehicles and furniture. They also may owe money to doctors, dentists and local utility companies. And of course, many people owe debts on their credit cards.

When recording your liabilities, you should use the amount that would be required to pay the debt off today. Do not simply add up the remaining payments, as they include interest charges that are not yet owed. You might need to contact your lender for the specific pay-off amount.

Liabilities are divided according to the amount of time remaining until the debt must be repaid, and they are categorized as either short-term or long-term debts. Credit cards debts are included as short-term debts because the goal is to get them paid off as fast as possible.

The next two worksheets will help you list your liabilities. The information you will need comes from *Action Module 1B: Your Debt Inventory* that you prepared in Chapter 1.

Worksheet 2D: Short-term Liabilities

Short-term debts must be repaid within one year.

Worksheet 2D | Short-term Liabilities

Short-term Liabilities	$ Amount
Credit Card #1	
Credit Card #2	
Credit Card #3	
Medical #1	
Medical #2	
Past-due Utility Bills	
Other Short-term Liabilities	
TOTAL SHORT-TERM LIABILITIES	

This worksheet is available for download at www.creditbooster.com/downloads/.

Worksheet 2E: Long-term Liabilities

Long-term debts will take one or more years to be repaid.

Worksheet 2E | Long-term Liabilities

Long-term Liabilities	$ Amount
Vehicle Loan #1	
Vehicle Loan #2	
Mortgage on 1st Residence	
2nd Mortgage on 1st Residence	
Mortgage on 2nd Residence	
Personal Loan #1	
Personal Loan #2	
Other Long-term Liabilities	
TOTAL LONG-TERM LIABILITIES	

This worksheet is available for download at www.creditbooster.com/downloads/.

Your Net Worth!

At the end of every year, corporations prepare a balance sheet. They use it to report everything they own and what they owe. The difference represents the total value of the shareholders' ownership in the company. The purpose of the balance sheet is to let their shareholders know the value of the company in dollars and cents.

Your household is like a company. You buy and sell things (including your time) and do work around the house in order to produce the things you need. So just like a company, you should also have a balance sheet. The result when you subtract your liabilities from your assets is your net worth.

Your net worth changes every day. Assets go up and down in value. Some assets, such as furniture or clothing, are used up over time. Your debts also go up and down (hopefully down).

Here are some examples of how net worth can be improved over time:

- Paying down debts
- Owning assets that go up in value
- Saving.

Here are some examples of how net worth can go down over time:

- Borrowing money
- Owning assets that go down in value
- Spending more than your income.

Many people make mistakes when thinking about improving their net worth. For example, you should understand that paying off a loan by taking money out of a saving account does not change net worth. It simply lowers the total of both assets and liabilities. Selling a car and putting the money in the bank does not immediately change net worth. Paying off one loan with another does not change net worth.

The ONLY way to improve net worth is to spend less than your income. Chapter 3 addresses income and spending.

What You Can Do!

Action Module 2: Calculating Your Net Worth

The five worksheets above can be compiled into one document that you can use to determine your net worth. What will you find out? The basic result of calculating your net worth is seeing whether or not you are solvent. Being solvent means that you could sell everything you own and have enough money to pay off all your debts. Being insolvent means that you would still owe money after selling everything.

So, which is it for you? Let's take a look. Use *Action Module 2: Your Net Worth* to calculate your net worth.

Action Module 2 | Your Net Worth

To calculate your net worth you should

Add your total assets:

Your Monetary Assets *(from Worksheet 2A)* _____

Your Tangible Assets *(from Worksheet 2B)* _____

Your Investment Assets *(from Worksheet 2C)* _____

Total Assets _____

Add your total liabilities:

Your Short-term Liabilities *(from Worksheet 2D)* _____

Your Long-term Liabilities *(from Worksheet 2E)* _____

Total Liabilities _____

Subtract your **Total Liabilities** from your **Total Assets** to get your Net Worth:

Total Assets _____

– Total Liabilities _____

= Net Worth _____

This worksheet is available for download at www.creditbooster.com/downloads/.

So, what did you find out? Are you solvent or insolvent? Being insolvent is not necessarily an immediate problem if you can handle the payments on your debts out of your income. And being solvent is not all that reassuring if your debt payments leave little extra to live on each month.

The real benefit from knowing your net worth is that it serves as a benchmark to track your financial progress. By spending less than you bring in each month you will see your net worth grow month after month and year after year. Using credit usually means that you are spending more each month than your income. That is no way to build net worth.

Summary

- Your attempts to improve your credit standing should begin with a realistic assessment of your current financial status.

- Your assets are the things you own as measured by their fair market value.

- Your liabilities are your debts as measured by the amount it would take to pay them off today.

- Your net worth is the difference between your assets and liabilities.

- You are solvent if your assets exceed your debts and insolvent if your liabilities exceed your assets.

- The only way to grow your net worth is to spend less than your income.

- You cannot borrow your way to a higher net worth.

The goal of this section is to provide you with a realistic picture of your financial status. In this chapter, we helped you identify and calculate your current net worth, a basic element of your financial health that is based on your assets and liabilities. In Chapter 3 we will help you determine the basics of your cash flow, in terms of your income and your expenses. In Chapter 4 you'll then use what you've learned so you can "*make sense of your financial situation.*"

In this chapter, we will help you determine the basics of your cash flow, as measured in terms of your income and your expenses.

What You Need To Know!

Chapter 2 told you precisely where you stand financially—What you own and what you owe. Now you can turn your attention to information that really determines your financial success—What you earn and what you spend. Do you spend more than you earn? Or is it the other way around?

This chapter addresses these questions and more. It will allow you to determine if your financial behavior is allowing you to get ahead or whether you are falling further and further behind.

Many people who want to change their financial and credit status think first about setting up a budget. Budgets are definitely a good idea, but budgets need to be based in on a realistic assessment. You need to look back before you can look ahead.

The key to financial success is spending less than you earn. That means saving. Saving should be something you do on a regular basis. An important philosophy in personal financial planning is to "pay yourself first." This means that saving is planned and occurs at the beginning of the month—not the end of the month. If you wait to see how much money will be left over, none will be left over. Your credit will improve considerably if you have money saved in bank accounts, retirement accounts and other places.

This chapter focuses on:

- Your **income** from all sources
- Your **expenses**
- Your **net gain** (or **net loss**), which is the difference between the two.

Again, you might be reassured by what you find in this chapter; you might find out that your fears are well founded; you might even learn that things are worse than you thought.

No matter. Simply knowing where your money is coming from and going is a good thing. This is because worry does not solve problems. *Action solves problems.* And action begins with a clear understanding of reality.

Your Income!

It may seem simple enough to determine your income. But it is easy to overlook things. **Income** is money that comes into your household from outside sources. For most people that means income from a job. But income can come from government benefits, interest from bank accounts, dividends from investments, pension income, garage sales, selling items on eBay, babysitting, and, even, gifts.

Worksheet 3A: Total Income

Worksheet 3A: Total Income will help you determine your income from all sources. In order to complete the worksheet, you will need to go back over your records. Ideally, you would want to complete a worksheet for the most recent year. But, to save time and keep things simple you could just focus on the most recent month.

Search all sources of information to find out all of your income. Think hard about where a few extra dollars might have come from last month. Perhaps ask family members, too. Then write those figures in the "$ Amount" column. Adding all the amounts reveals "Total Income."

Next, you will find it helpful to also calculate the percentage of your income that comes from the various sources. Once you add up all your income, that amount equals 100%. To calculate each income amount as a percentage, you divide each income item by total income and multiply it by 100. This process is not complicated, as you will see.

For example, if your total income is $3000 per month and gross salary (before taxes and other withholdings) in "Gross Salary #1" is $2700, divide the $2700 by $3000. Now you know that 90% ($2700/$3000 x 100) of your total income comes from that source.

Worksheet 3A | Total Income

Income	$ Amount	% of Total Income
Gross Salary #1		
Gross Salary #2		
Gross Salary #3		
Social Security Benefits #1		
Social Security Benefits #2		
Interest Income		
Annunity Income		
Pension Benefits		
Dividend Income		
Gifts		
Other		
TOTAL INCOME		100%

This worksheet is available for download at www.creditbooster.com/downloads/.

What You Spend!

If you are like most people, you have a general idea of how much money you spend each month. But many of the details may be unclear. Some expense items, like rent, may be the same each month. Other item amounts vary up and down. And some special expenses, such as auto insurance, occur in some months but not others.

The next two worksheets will help you determine your spending. The information you will need to complete the worksheets can come from your checkbook, receipts you have kept on file and the various bills you receive. If you have maintained good financial records (perhaps by putting them into a box), you can be fairly accurate when filling out the worksheet.

When the exact information is not available, you might need to create some estimates. Many people find it beneficial to keep track of every dollar spent for a whole month by writing each amount down. Then the next month you can complete the worksheet again and get a very accurate picture of what you spend.

Expenses should be divided into two groups: fixed and variable expenses. Fixed expenses stay the same (or nearly so) each month. Usually there is not much you can do to reduce the cost of these items, such as rent or car payment. Variable expenses change from month to month. Many of these amounts can be reduced if necessary, like spending on food and entertainment. Variable expenses are the first place to look when you need to reduce spending. Some variable expenses, however, cannot be reduced without major impacts on your life, such as gasoline for your car. People with high fixed expenses who must reduce spending will have a tough time doing so. For example, getting out of a monthly car payment means selling the vehicle.

Worksheet 3B: Fixed Expenses

Worksheet 3B: Fixed Expenses can be used to list your fixed expenses. Again, you should write in the amount for each fixed expense item and add them up to obtain your total fixed expenses. Then, to calculate each fixed expense amount as a percentage of your income, you divide each item by total income (not total fixed expenses) and multiply it by 100.

For example, if your rent payment is $900 per month and gross salary (before taxes and other withholdings) in "Gross Salary #1" is $3000, divide the $900 by $3000. Now you know that 30% ($900/$3000 x 100) of your total income is used to pay your rent.

Worksheet 3B | Fixed Expenses

Fixed Expenses	$ Amount	% of Total Income (fill in total income)
Fixed Savings		
Rent or Mortgage Payment		
Homeowner's Insurance (if not in morgage)		
Automobile Insurance - Car #1		
Automobile Insurance - Car #2		
Life Insurance		
Health Insurance		
Other Insurance		
Federal Income Taxes		
Social Security Taxes		
State Income Taxes		
Local Income Taxes		
Personal Property Taxes		
Cable TV Base Charge		
Internet Access		
Cell Phone #1 Base Charge		
Charitable Donations		
Loan Payment #1		

(continued)

(continued)

Fixed Expenses	$ Amount	% of Total Income (fill in total income)
Loan Payment #2		
Loan Payment #3		
Loan Payment #4		
Other Fixed Expenses		
Other Fixed Expenses		
TOTAL FIXED EXPENSES		

This worksheet is available for download at www.creditbooster.com/downloads/.

Worksheet 3C: Variable Expenses

Worksheet 3C: Variable Expenses can be used to list your variable expenses. Again, you should write in the amount for each variable expense item and add them up to obtain your total variable expenses. Then, to calculate each variable expense amount as a percentage of your income, you divide each item by total income (not total variable expenses) and multiply it by 100.

For example, if your Food (at home) expense is $600 per month and gross salary (before taxes and other withholdings) in "Gross Salary #1" is $3000, divide the $600 by $3000. Now you know that 20% ($600/$3000 x 100) of your total income is goes toward food consumed at home.

Worksheet 3C | Variable Expenses

Variable Expenses	$ Amount	% of Total Income _____ (fill in total income)
Variable Savings*		
Food (at home)		
Food (away from home)		
Utilities		
Cable TV Pay Per View		
Cell Phone Extra Minutes		
Cell Phone Roaming Fees		
Household Operations		
Gasoline, oil, vehicle maintenance		
Medical Expenses		
Medicines		

(continued)

(continued)

Variable Expenses	$ Amount	% of Total Income (fill in total income)
Clothing and upkeep		
Credit Card Payment #1		
Credit Card Payment #2		
Credit Card Payment #3		
Credit Card Payment #4		
Entertainment		
Gifts		
Personal Allowances		
Personal Care		
Charitable Contributions		
Miscellaneous		
Other Variable Expenses		
Other Variable Expenses		
TOTAL VARIABLE EXPENSES		

This worksheet is available for download at www.creditbooster.com/downloads/.

Remember that a very important rule in personal financial planning is to "pay yourself first." This means that saving is an item of expense just like any other. It is not what you have left over. That is why savings was included as an expense in the worksheets above. But saving is part of any net gain and can be added back. It is how you get ahead. In fact, it is the only way to get ahead.

Your Net Gain!

At the end of every year, corporations prepare an income and expense statement. The purpose is to determine if they made a profit for the year.

Your household is like a company. In a very real sense, you want to make a profit. You can call this profit your **net gain**. If you have a net gain it means that you reported more income than what you spent during the month or year. Similarly, if you spent more than your income, resulting in a **net loss** for a month or year, you would have to borrow money or take money out of your savings to make ends meet. This means you would have less money or more debt at the end of the month or year.

What You Can Do!

Action Module 3: Your Net Gain / Loss

The three worksheets above tell you if you are spending more than your income. This information is key to boosting your credit standing. If you are spending more than your income, you are falling deeper and deeper into debt. Did you have a net gain or loss last month? Are you getting ahead financially? Let's take a look.

To calculate your net gain/loss:

1. Enter your Total Income here (from *Worksheet 3A*)

2. Add your Fixed Expenses (from *Worksheet 3B*) to your Variable Expenses

   (from *Worksheet 3C*)

   _____   +   _____   =   _____

3. Subtract #2 from #1   −   _____

4. Add back to #3 any Fixed or Variable Savings   +   _____

   Net Gain (or Loss)   =   _____

The real benefit of the worksheet is that it focuses on reality. The statement tells you exactly what you have been doing. Thus, it serves as a basis for future actions. What does that mean? It means that you must begin to think of ways to increase income and/or reduce spending. To help you get started, take a few minutes to write down in **Worksheet 3D: Three Ways I Could Increase Income** and in **Worksheet 3E: Five Ways I Could Reduce Spending**. Then, we'll use the next two chapters to build on these ideas.

Worksheet 3D | Three Ways I Could Increase Income

Idea #1		
Idea #2		
Idea #3		

This worksheet is available for download at www.creditbooster.com/downloads/.

Worksheet 3E | Five Ways I Could Reduce Spending

Idea #1		
Idea #2		
Idea #3		
Idea #4		
Idea #5		

This worksheet is available for download at www.creditbooster.com/downloads/

Summary

- Improving your financial condition and, thus, your credit history requires that you look back to previous financial behavior.

- Your income and expense statement provides a summary of your financial activities over a prior month or year.

- Income includes all financial inflows for your household.

- Fixed expenses are predictable but difficult to reduce.

- Variable expenses are unpredictable but can sometimes be reduced if necessary.

- The only way to grow your net worth is to have net gains on your income and expense statements—spend less than you earn.

The goal of this section is to provide you with a realistic picture of your financial status. In this chapter, we helped you determine the basics of your cash flow, as measured in terms of your income and your expenses. In Chapter 4 you'll then use what you've learned so you can *make sense of your financial situation.*

In this chapter we will use what you've learned about the basics of your cash flow, in terms of your income and your expenses, so you can "make sense of your financial situation."

What You Need To Know!

At this point you might be asking yourself why we have been focusing on your finances when this book is about boosting your credit status. The answer is simple. Lenders focus on this same information. They want to know what you own and to whom you owe money and how much. They want to know how much money you make and spend. They want to know if you can afford the payments on any additional credit that you are granted.

Anything you can do to enhance your net worth and spend less than you earn on a monthly basis will enhance your standing with lenders. But lenders look even deeper. They use the information that you provide about your finances to make comparisons among your assets, debts, income and expenses. These comparisons, called financial ratios, more clearly indicate your credit worthiness.

Financial ratios are calculations that help you assess your financial condition. Ratios can serve as yardsticks to help you understand your spending and credit-usage patterns. This chapter focuses on the most important of these yardsticks. Using the information from Chapters 2 and 3 you will calculate your own ratios and compare the results to those desired by lenders.

#1 How Long Could You Make It Without Income?

You can use the **Basic Liquidity Ratio** to determine the number of months that you could meet your monthly expenses should all income cease. In other words, how long could you survive without income before you had to sell things or cash in your investments?

BASIC LIQUIDITY RATIO

Your basic liquidity ratio is:

Monetary assets (*from **Worksheet 2A***) _____

Divided by

Total Monthly Expenses (*from Step #2*, ***Action Module 3***) _____

Basic Liquidity Ratio = _____

For example, if your monetary assets were $4000 and your monthly expenses were $2000, then your basic liquidity ratio would be two months:

$$\frac{\$4000}{\$2000} = 2$$

#2 Do Your Assets Exceed Your Debts?

The **asset-to-debt** ratio compares your total assets with total liabilities. It provides you with a broad measure of your financial solvency. An asset-to-debt ratio over 1.0 shows that you own more than you owe.

ASSET-TO-DEBT RATIO

Your asset-to-debt ratio is:

Total assets (*from Step #1*, ***Action Module 2***) _____

Divided by

Total Liabilities (*from Step #2*, ***Action Module 2***) _____

Asset-to-Debt Ratio = _____

For example, if your total assets were $80,000 and your total debts $40,000, your assets-to-debt ratio would be 2, indicating that you own twice as much as you owe:

$$\frac{\$8000}{\$40,000} = 2$$

#3 Is Your Take-home Pay High Enough to Make Your Non-mortgage Debt Payments?

The **debt payments-to-take-home-pay** ratio divides your monthly debt repayments (excluding mortgage debt) by your monthly take-home pay (not gross income). Take-home pay is the amount of your income remaining after taxes and withholding for such purposes as insurance and union dues. Mortgage debt is excluded because buying a home is also an investment. This ratio tells you if your monthly payments for debts other than your mortgage are too high.

DEBT PAYMENTS-TO-TAKE-HOME-PAY RATIO

Your debt payments-to-take-home-pay is:

Total non-mortgage debt payments (*total of Loans and Credit Card payments from* **Worksheets 3B** *and* **3C**)   _____

Divided by

Monthly take-home pay (*total Monthly Income minus federal, state and local income taxes, Social Security Taxes and other items subtracted from your gross pay, from* **Worksheets 3A, 3B,** *and* **3C**)   _____

= Debt Payment-to-Take-Home-Pay Ratio   _____

For example, if your monthly take home pay is $2000 and you have non-mortgage debt payments of $500 per month, the ratio is .25 or 25%. This means that 25% of your take-home pay goes towards debts other than your mortgage.

$$\frac{\$500}{\$2,000} = .25$$

#4 Is Your Total Income High Enough to Make All Your Debt Payments?

The **debt service-to-gross income** ratio compares the dollars you spend on monthly debt repayments (including mortgages) with gross monthly income. It tells you if your total monthly debt payments including your mortgage are too high.

DEBT SERVICE-TO-GROSS INCOME RATIO

Your debt service-to-income ratio is:

Total monthly debt payments (*Total of mortgage, loan and credit card payments, from* **Worksheets 3B** *and* **3C**) _____

Divided by

Total Monthly Income (*from* **Action Module 3**) _____

Debt Service-to-Income Ratio = _____

For example, if your total debts payments for the month are $1,000 and your total monthly income was $3,000, your debt service-to-income ratio would be .33 or 33%. This means that 33% of your gross income is needed to pay your debts each month.

$$\frac{\$1,000}{\$3,000} = .33$$

#5 Are You Saving Enough?

As noted earlier, the only way to build your net worth is to spend less than your income. Or, simply put, you must save. How do you know if you are saving enough? Or even what you are saving? The savings ratio compares your dollars saved to your after-tax income.

SAVINGS RATIO

Your savings ratio is:

Total Savings (*from Worksheets 3B and 3C; can also include amounts your employer is contributing to your retirement plan.*)   _____

Divided by

Total after-tax income (*Total monthly income minus federal, state and local income taxes, and Social Security taxes from Worksheets 3A, 3B and 3C*)   _____

Savings Ratio   =   _____

For example, if your after-tax income is $2,500 per month and you are saving $250 per month, your savings ratio is 0.10 or 10 percent. This means that you are saving 10% of your after-tax income each month.

$$\frac{\$250}{\$2,500} = .10$$

What You Can Do!

Action Module 4.1

Now that you have calculated your ratios, let's look at what the information might mean to lenders.

RATIO #1: My Basic Liquidity Ratio Is _____.

Most financial experts recommend that people have monetary assets equal to three months' expenses in emergency cash reserves. That means your Basic Liquidity Ratio should be at least 3.

Of course, the exact amount of monetary assets necessary depends on your family situation and your job. A smaller ratio may be sufficient for your needs if you have very steady income and are very unlikely to be laid off. You would also need ample sick days and a good disability income insurance plan.

Households dependent on the income from a self-employed person with fluctuating income need a larger emergency cash reserve.

Households with two earners are protected a bit if this ratio is too low. But the loss of one income will still require a big cutback in spending if there are too few cash reserves set aside.

RATIO #2: My Asset-to-Debt Ratio Is _____.

If you owe more than you own, then you are technically insolvent. This would true if your asset-to-debt ratio is below 1.0. You can be insolvent even if your income is enough to pay your current debts on time. Young individuals and families often have asset-to-debt ratios under 2.0. As people get older this ratio usually improves.

RATIO #3: My Debt Payments-to-Take-Home-Pay Ratio Is _____.

Many lenders feel that a person is too far in debt if his or her debt payments-to-take home pay ratio is 20 percent or more. If your ratio exceeds this figure, you would be in serious financial trouble if a disruption in income occurs.

Recall that mortgage payments are not included in this ratio. A figure of 20 percent or more means that a too high a percentage of your income is going for car loans, credit card debt, student loans, furniture and appliance debt and other personal debts.

RATIO #4: My Debt Service-to-Gross Income Ratio Is _____.

Many lenders, especially mortgage lenders, include mortgage payments in their assessment of someone's credit worthiness. They use the debt service-to-gross income ratio to make this judgment. A ratio of 36% or more indicates that gross income is inadequate to make debt repayments, including housing costs. People with ratios exceeding this figure have little flexibility in their budget.

Mortgage payments often exceed thirty percent of the typical family's gross income. That means that there is little room left over for car loan debt, credit card debt and other personal debts. People who have high levels of such debt payments often have trouble obtaining a mortgage to buy a home. Similarly, people who have high mortgage payments may have difficulty obtaining other types of loans.

RATIO #5: My Savings Ratio Is _____.

Financial experts often recommend that people save 15 to 20 percent of their gross income. This figure would include any funds going into a retirement account and would include their employer's contributions into such an account. Young families need to be saving about 12 percent just for retirement. That leaves 3 to 8 percent for other savings needs. The average American is saving less than 3% in TOTAL. Clearly, this is an area in need of improvement for many people.

Action Module 4.2: Financial Ratios Summary

Do any of your ratios appear to be too low? The column on the left below lists come ideas for how you can improve one or more of your ratios. The numbers in parentheses indicate which ratios would be improved if you put the suggestions into action. On the right you can write in the specific actions you can take. For example, you might want to build an emergency fund to improve your basic liquidity ratio. If so, you would indicate in the box on the right the specific amount you will put away monthly to achieve this goal.

Action Module 4.2 | Financial Ratios Summary

What I *Could* Do To Boost My Ratios	What I *Will* Do To Boost My Basic Liquidity Ration
Cut some spending so you can put extra money into an emergency fund *(Ratio#1, Ratio #2, and Ratio #5)*	
Investigate the disability income insurance available through your employer. *(Ratio #1)*	
Reduce some of the savings you are already doing and earmark those funds for an emergency fund *(Ratio #1)*	
Focus on debt reduction by picking one debt to pay off as soon as possible *(Ratio #3 and Ratio #4)*	
Sell some assets and use the funds to pay off a debt. Perhaps you have some used furniture, old computers or other household goods that could be sold *(Ratio #3 and Ratio #4)*	
Take a second job for several months and put all of the extra income towards debt repayment. Or just put the money in the bank to build your monetary assets *(Ratio #1 and Ratio #2)*	
Contact a not-for-profit credit counseling service to see if a debt management program is right for you. *(Ratio #2 and Ratio #3)*	
Cut spending to build up additional monetary assets. *(Ratio #1 and Ratio #2)*	
Refinance your mortgage to obtain a lower interest rate and thus a lower monthly payment *(Ratio #4)*	
Other ideas?	

This worksheet is available for download at www.creditbooster.com/downloads/.

As you developed the list of things to do in the column on the right, it probably became clear that you are going to have to change your spending habits and, perhaps, find more income. Making the list was easy. Taking the actions will require specific targets for you to shoot for.

Summary

- Knowing basic information about how much you own and owe and earn and spend can help your efforts to improve your credit status. Even more insight can be achieved if you use this basic information to calculate several financial ratios that lenders often use to assess credit applicants.

- The basic liquidity ratio tells you if you have enough money set aside to meet financial emergencies and get through a period of unemployment.

- The asset-to-debt ratio tells you if you own more than you owe.

- The debt payments-to-take-home-pay ratio tells you if your monthly payments for debts other than your mortgage are too high.

- The debt service-to-gross income ratio tells you if your total monthly debt payments including your mortgage are too high.

- The savings ratio tells you if you are saving enough.

Later, in Chapter 8, you will develop those specific income and spending targets by developing a budget.

Section III: Assessing Your Debt Status will next outline how your financial/credit status is assessed in standard measures that lenders can use to determine whether or not to extend you additional credit. Let's move on now to *Chapter 5: Understanding Your Credit Report and Your Credit History*, which explains how your credit history is recorded in a formal credit reporting system.

Chapter 5 | Understanding Your Credit Report and Your Credit History

In *Section III: Assessing Your Debt Status* we outline how your financial/credit status is assessed in standard measures that others can use to determine whether or not to extend you additional credit. This chapter explains how your credit history is recorded in a formal credit reporting system.

What You Need To Know!

Your Credit History and Rating

Lenders want to know how their potential customers have managed their credit in the past. Why? Because, they need to determine whether or not someone they may loan money to is likely to repay it. If a potential borrower has made timely credit repayments in the past, he or she is likely to do so again. Thus, lenders make use of **credit bureaus** that gather from banks and other credit grantors information on your credit usage and other financial behaviors.

Your credit history at the various credit bureaus contains:

- A listing of past and present credit accounts
- A record of whether those accounts were or are being paid on-time
- Notes on if and when debts were referred to collection agencies
- Record of all negative credit entries that goes back seven years. Bankruptcies will show for ten years.

Your credit history is doubly important because companies, such as life and automobile insurance companies, landlords and potential employers, may use it to assess your risk factor.

The Big Three Credit Bureaus

There are three major credit bureaus: Experian®, Equifax and TransUnion™. Actually, there are hundreds of other local and regional credit reporting agencies, but each receives information from one of these three major bureaus.

> **Your credit history may NOT be exactly the same at each bureau.**

These companies make money by providing credit information to banks, mortgage lenders, employers, and loan and credit card companies. They are competitors and do not share information. Thus, your credit history may not be exactly the same with each company. For that reason, it is very important that you review your credit reports from all three major credit bureaus.

What's in a Credit Report?

A credit report is a record of your personal credit history. Because of the extensive information contained in a credit report, creditors turn to it first when deciding whether or not to grant credit. Your credit report DOES NOT contain your race, religion, or political preference. But it will contain information on:

- **PERSONAL IDENTIFIERS** – This section includes your name, past and present addresses, previous employers, current employers and your Social Security Number (SSN).

- **CREDIT ACCOUNTS** – This section includes information on current and past loans and credit accounts, credit limits, current balances and payment histories. Payment history includes late payments, repossessions, charge-offs, and collection activity.

- **PUBLIC RECORD INFORMATION** – This section includes information about any tax liens, bankruptcies, or legal judgments in lawsuits against you.

- **INQUIRIES** – This section includes information about businesses that have requested your credit report within the last 12 months.

- **NEGATIVE INFORMATION** – To assist you in reading the report, some credit reports may add a section that summarizes all negative information.

Why Should You Review Your Credit Report?

Studies by consumer protection agencies as well as the Federal Trade Commission show that *more than half* of all credit reports contain errors.

> **Most credit reports contain mistakes, which could require you to pay higher interest rates and perhaps prevent you from getting credit in the future.**

Credit bureaus are not motivated to be positive that your credit report is 100 percent accurate. They merely list the data that has been reported to them by creditors. That leads to several common mistakes that could affect your credit history:

- **CONFUSION OVER YOUR NAME** – Perhaps you entered Bob Jones on one application and Robert Jones on the others.

- **WRONG PERSON** – Your credit report may contain information on a person with a similar name.

- **BUREAU ERROR** – Some bureaus transcribe your information from tapes or written reports. If the transcriber makes a typographical error or misreads a number, it will show on your credit report.

- **CREDITOR ERROR** – The creditor that provided the information to the bureau did not transcribe the data correctly before sending it.

- **INCOMPLETE DATA** – Since the three major credit bureaus do not share information and since they only receive information from creditors who subscribe to their services, it is likely that some good credit information will never be reported to one or more credit bureaus.

For these reasons, it is very important that you check your credit report before making a significant purchase on credit. Many people check their credit history once a year. You will learn how to analyze your credit report and fix mistakes in the following chapters.

Possible Credit Report Problems

In addition to the errors that often occur in credit reports, your own credit behavior in the past may have led to negative information being recorded in your file. Lenders decide what behaviors to report. So it might be that a behavior you feel was unimportant may have been reported negatively. OR, a behavior you thought was important may not have been deemed so by a lender and went unreported.

Worksheet 5A can be used to record situations that you recall in your current or past credit usage that might have affected your credit history. What bad credit might be in your past? Overdue bills? Medical bills turned over to creditors? What concerns you about your credit? List those situations below.

Worksheet 5A | My List of Possible Credit Report Problems

Situation	Creditor	When
Example: Late car payments three months in a row	*Jamestown Bank*	*Jan. - Mar. 2006*

This worksheet is available for download at www.creditbooster.com/downloads/

> **YOU are responsible for the accuracy of your credit report.**

You are ultimately responsible for the accuracy of the information in your credit report. Each month, credit bureaus receive millions of pieces of data on credit, so it's easy to understand how mistakes can be made. Credit bureaus are, however, legally obligated to investigate disputed information and correct errors you bring to their attention.

Obtaining Your Credit Reports

Getting your credit report is easy. The Federal Fair and Accurate Credit Transactions (FACT) Act of 2003 allows consumers to obtain one free credit report from each of the three major bureaus every year. These three agencies have established a central source for obtaining your free reports. This central source is available on the Internet at **www.annualcreditreport.com**. Note that there are a number of similar addresses on the Internet. Many are sites that offer various services at a cost to you. You should make certain that you use only the central source web address. When you order, you will need to provide your:

- Full name (with Sr., Jr., III)
- Current address
- Previous addresses within the last five years
- Social Security Number
- Birth date
- Telephone number.

Those who do not have access to the Internet can order their free reports by calling 877-322-8228 toll-free. (TDD service for the hearing impaired is available at 877-730-4104.) You will be asked a series of questions to verify your identity and your report will be mailed to you.

You may also be able to obtain a free copy of your credit report if you meet any one of the following criteria:

- You've been denied credit, insurance, or employment in the past 60 days and the information in it was part of the reason your request was denied

- You're on welfare
- Your credit report is inaccurate because of fraud.

Understand that the big three credit bureaus DO NOT routinely share information with each other, though their sources of information are similar. One credit report may or may not contain exactly the same information as another. Therefore, you'll need to *review all three* annually to be sure each is accurate. If you have not viewed a copy of your credit report for several years it is a good idea to request a free report from all three bureaus. Then, one year later you can request a report from one of the bureaus, four months after that request a free report from another bureau, and four months after that request a report from the third bureau. In this way you are checking at least one of your reports every four months, allowing you to catch errors early.

Beware of offers from other companies and web sites that advertise they can obtain your credit report for free. These free offers are not direct requests for a report from one of the three national agencies. Instead these firms obtain your permission to request a report that they then send to you. The company then will add your name and other data to their files that they later sell for solicitation purposes. In effect, you are paying for nothing. With most of these "free" offers you are automatically signed up for a free 30-day trial membership in a credit report information service. You must cancel within the thirty-days or your credit card will be assessed the annual membership fee of upwards of $100 or more.

So, do not use free credit report offers from companies other than the three national bureaus via the official web address or phone number listed here. Note, also, that each of the three national bureaus offers various credit report monitoring services for a fee on their web sites. These services provide reports more regularly than the annual free reports.

Sample Credit Report

The information in a credit report falls into several sections, depending on which credit bureau supplies the report. Reports prepared by different credit bureaus may state similar information in different sections. Let's look at these sample pages from a credit report and see what we can learn.

Sample Account Summary Page

Credit Report For:

John C. Jones
123 Elm Street
Central City, MI 48310

SS# 333-99-8888
670-324-5789

ABC Bank MasterCard
PO Box XXXX
Wilmington, DE 19850

Creditor's name

Account Number: 1234567890123456

Account Status: Open

Past due 30 days.

$20 past due as of 04/2002.

Details: As of 04/2009, this account is scheduled to go to a positive status.

Date Opened: 05/1999

Reported Since: 05/1999

Date of Status: 04/2002

Last Reported: 04/2002

Type Credit: Revolving

Terms: NA

Monthly Payment: 20

Responsibility: Joint

Credit Limit/Original Amount: $5000

High Balance: $5,344

Recent Balance: $5,344 (as of 04/30/2002)

Recent Payment: 0

What this statement says is that this account was overdue by 30 days in 04/2002. It's a credit card with a minimum payment of $20. Terms are NA (not applicable) because it is revolving credit without a fixed number of payments. (An installment loan would have the remaining number of payments listed under terms.)

You can see this consumer is over the maximum credit limit and missed the 04/2002 payment. This may trigger late payment penalties and a higher interest rate on the balance.

Sample Public Information Page

Source:	Date filed/discharged:	Ownership:	Claim:	Comments:
Howard County Dist Ct 301 Main Street. Fort Worth, TX 76110 **File:** TX938575	03/2001, NA	Joint	$7,456	Staus: civil claim judgment filed Plantiff: AA Auto Credit This item will continue on record until 03/2008. This item was verified on 09/2001 and remained unchanged

In this sample public information page, AA Auto Credit has filed a claim in Howard County District Court for the amount of $7,456 against this consumer. This negative entry will be removed in 03/2008.

| Howard County Dist Ct
301 Main Street.
Fort Worth, TX 76110

File: TX701343 | 10/2001, 01/2002 | Joint | $48,943 | Status: Chapter 7 bankruptcy discharged. This item will continue on record until 10/2011 This item was verified on 03/2002 and remained unchanged |

This couple filed jointly for chapter 7 bankruptcy in 10/2001 to discharge debts totaling $48,943. This negative entry will be on their credit report for ten years from date filed or 10/2011

If you have problems understanding a particular entry, call the credit bureau and request an explanation. Credit bureaus are required by law to explain information on your report that you don't understand. Be aware, though, that sometimes it may take awhile to get an answer to your question when you call. You might try calling during off-peak hours for faster service. Also, credit bureaus are required to explain what an entry means, but not why an entry exists on your credit report. Remember, the credit bureau only compiles information from your creditors. If it is an error, you will learn how to fix it in the next chapter.

You may be surprised to find negative information about loans you took out several years ago. Fortunately, most negative entries will not stay on your credit report forever. Here is a list of the time limits, after which the credit bureau should remove the negative item from your credit history.

Sample Credit Information Page							
Company Name: AAA-1 Bank Account Number: 12345	**Ownership:** Joint	**Account Dates:** Date Opened 10/1993 Last Activity 04/2002	**Type of Account and Status:** Revolving Past Due	**Balance:** Highest $4,777 Current $4,536	**Remaining Payments:** 0	**Past Due:** $60	**Date Reported:** 04/2002
Superior Auto Credit Account Number: 42332	Individual	Date Opened 04/2000 Last Activity 02/2002	Installment Repossessed	Highest $18,500 Current $14 345	36	$14,345	02/2002

> **Most negative data is kept for seven years;**
> **bankruptcies are kept for ten years.**

Most negative information should be removed from your credit report seven years after the last transaction in the account. However, there are several exceptions:

- Bankruptcies are kept for ten years.

- Lawsuits or judgments you have not paid are reported until the statute of limitations runs out or seven years, whichever is longer.

- Any negative information, regardless of how old it is, can be included when you
    - Apply for a loan of more than $150,000.
    - Apply for a job with a salary of $75,000 or more.
    - Apply for $150,000 or more in life insurance.

What You Can Do!

Action Module 5

When you receive your credit reports from the three national credit bureaus you will want to examine them carefully to make sure they are accurate and up-to-date. There are three basic errors that can occur:

1. **MISSING ACCOUNT INFORMATION** – Accounts that you do have now (or have had in the past) but which have not been included in your report. This can occur because not all lenders report information to all three bureaus.

2. **ACCOUNTS WITH ERRORS** – Accounts that you do have now (or have had in the past) that are included in the report but which contain erroneous or inaccurate information. Such inaccuracies can be relatively simple errors such as reporting a joint account in only one person's name. Or they can be major errors such as showing an account as unpaid when in fact it is up-to-date.

3. **WRONG ACCOUNTS** – Accounts shown in your name that you do not now have nor have ever had in your name.

The following worksheets can be used to summarize the errors you find in your credit reports. Download fullsize worksheets at www.creditbooster.com.

Action Module 5A | Equifax Credit Report Summary Sheets

My Equifax Credit Report	
My Accounts Missing from the Report	
Name of Account	Type of Account, Date Opened, Current Status
My Accounts Reported but with Errors	
Name of Account	Nature of the Error
Accounts Reported That Are Not My Accounts	
Name of Account	Type of Account, Date Allegedly Opened, Current Status

This worksheet is available for download at www.creditbooster.com/downloads/

Action Module 5B | TransUnion™ Credit Report Summary Sheets

My TransUnion™ Credit Report	
My Accounts Missing from the Report	
Name of Account	Type of Account, Date Opened Current Status
My Accounts Reported but with Errors	
Name of Account	Nature of the Error
Accounts Reported That Are Not My Accounts	
Name of Account	Type of Account, Date Allegedly Opened, Current Status

This worksheet is available for download at www.creditbooster.com/downloads/

Action Module 5C | Experian® Credit Report Summary Sheets

My Experian® Credit Report	
My Accounts Missing from the Report	
Name of Account	Type of Account, Date Opened Current Status
My Accounts Reported but with Errors	
Name of Account	Nature of the Error
Accounts Reported That Are Not My Accounts	
Name of Account	Type of Account, Date Allegedly Opened, Current Status

This worksheet is available for download at www.creditbooster.com/downloads/

Summary

- Improving your financial condition and, thus, your credit history requires that you find out what information is contained in your credit bureau files.

- There are three major, national credit bureaus and each may have differing information about your credit history.

- Everyone should obtain a copy of the credit reports once each year and examine the reports carefully for errors.

- Three major errors can occur in credit reports: accounts that are not listed, accounts that are listed but with inaccurate information about your history on the account, and accounts that are listed but that do not belong in your report.

Knowing the information in your credit reports is key to improving your credit status. Later, in Chapter 9, you will learn about the steps necessary to correct any errors. But first, you must also consider another major aspect of your credit reputation—your credit score. Credit scores are the focus of Chapter 6.

In *Assessing Your Debt Status*, Chapter 5 explained how your credit history is recorded in a formal credit reporting system. This chapter provides detail on the purpose of the credit score, which "measures" your credit history, how it is used by potential lenders, and how you can obtain those scores.

What You Need To Know!

You have been interested in buying a new car for some time. You see an ad in the paper for low 3.9% APR financing. So you go down to the dealer, pick out a vehicle, and apply for the loan.

Then you are told you do not qualify for the low rate and must pay 7.9% instead. Why? The dealer informs you that your credit score is too low.

Welcome to the world of credit scoring.

Recall from Chapter 5 that the three major credit bureaus monitor your every request for credit and every late or unpaid debt. They also look at the amount of debt you are carrying on your accounts even if they are being paid on time. This information is in your credit report.

But lenders are busy people. They cannot take time to analyze every line of your credit report, which might be several pages long. Instead, lenders use credit scoring to help determine if you are creditworthy.

What Is a Credit Score?

A credit score is a number lenders use to help them decide: "If I give this person a loan or credit card, how likely is it that I will get paid back on time?" A score is a snapshot of your credit risk picture at a particular point in time. People with lower scores are deemed to have a lower likelihood of repayment. They will pay higher interest rates or possibly be turned down altogether when they apply for credit.

Prior to development of credit scoring systems, approving credit was more subjective. In the old days, creditors had no way objectively and fairly to compare one person's credit application with that of another person. As a result, creditors often gave credit to people who perhaps should not have it, and many of those people defaulted on their loans. The lenders experienced higher delinquency rates than they would like, and this resulted in higher interest rates for everyone.

All three of the major credit reporting bureaus now calculate and report credit scores to lenders. You also have the right to know your scores. Although various brand names are used for the credit scoring systems, the most well known score was developed by Fair Isaac and Company. It is called the FICO® score.

Each credit bureau uses the FICO® scoring model, but each has its own name for the credit scores it uses:

Equifax = Beacon®
TransUnion™ = Empirica®
Experian® = Experian/Fair Isaac®

Any other score is not your FICO® score—rather it is a "FICO-like" score that may or may not be the same as your actual FICO® score. (Some of the information in this chapter was provided courtesy of the credit scoring experts at Fair Isaac and Company, Inc.)

Because your credit file at each of the three major credit bureaus may differ, your scores may differ as well.

Why Credit Scores Are Important Today!

As mentioned above, credit scores are important today because they affect your ability to get credit and the interest you will pay for the credit that you do get. Credit scores give lenders a fast, objective measurement of your credit risk. Before the use of scoring, the credit granting process could be slow, inconsistent and unfairly biased.

Credit scores have made big improvements in the credit-approval process. Lenders have made the information in your credit bureau files more important than ever before because the information in your credit bureau files is used to calculate your credit scores.

There's no one "score cutoff" used by all lenders telling them to deny or approve a loan. So it's hard to say whether your score is a good one or a bad one. Each lending situation is different. For example, a FICO® score of 750 may qualify you for a Platinum VISA credit card from the XYZ bank, whereas a score of 675 may indicate you're a better match for a standard card from the ABC bank. Your lender may be able to give you guidance on the criteria they use to approve for specific types of credit.

Here is a breakdown of FICO® scores for the general population that uses credit:

Percent of the Population	FICO® Score Range
Top 20%	Above 780
Next 20%	740-779
Middle 20%	690-739
Next 20%	620-689
Bottom 20%	Below 620

The following chart shows the likelihood that a person in various score ranges will become delinquent on a loan.

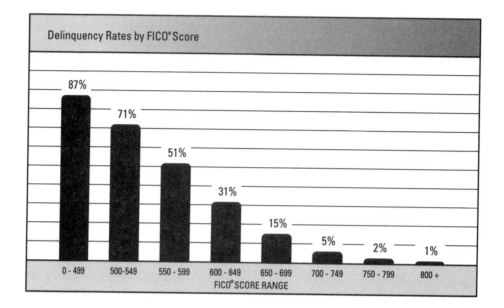

Delinquency Rates by FICO® Score

FICO® SCORE RANGE	Delinquency Rate
0 - 499	87%
500-549	71%
550 - 599	51%
600 - 649	31%
650 - 699	15%
700 - 749	5%
750 - 799	2%
800 +	1%

Under the concept of tiered interest, lenders offer lower interest rates to their customers with higher credit scores while charging steeper rates to more risky applicants. Note that even people with low credit scores usually can find some lender who will say "yes." Of course, the interest rate will be high for those borrowers. For this reason, you should always make sure that your credit bureau file is accurate before filing out a credit application.

Mortgage lenders set interest rates based on an applicant's credit score. Here are some illustrative credit scores and the corresponding interest rates and payments on a $216,000, thirty-year fixed rate home mortgage:

Credit Score	APR	Monthly Payment
760-850	5.85%	$1275
700-759	6.08%	$1306
680-699	6.25%	$1330
660-679	6.47%	$1361
640-659	6.90%	$1422
620-639	7.44%	$1502

As you can see, your credit score can mean hundreds of dollars per year and thousands of dollars over the life of a loan. The difference between a 5.85% APR and a 6.90% APR is $147 ($1,422 - $1,275) per month, $1,764 (12 x $147) per year, and $52,920 (30 x $1,764) over the life of the loan. These amounts are solely interest, as the amount of the loan remained the same in each case.

People with lower scores will be turned down or, commonly, referred to a lender in the sub-prime market. The sub-prime market is comprised of lenders who focus on higher-risk applicants. They charge commensurately higher interest rates as a result. Many applicants who are placed in this market are happy to have found a loan. However, many fail to realize that they would qualify for loans at standard rates if they had searched more extensively and undertook steps to improve their credit score.

Essentially, your credit score puts you into a grouping with other borrowers who have a similar chance of nonpayment. It does not mean that you personally have the same chance of nonpayment, but lenders cannot individualize down to that level. Instead, they use group averages. Things you can do to improve your credit score move you into a different group without necessarily changing your particular chance of nonpayment.

Credit cards are another area where credit scoring is important, and it's not just when you apply for a card. Most credit card issuers recheck their customers' credit reports and credit scores on a regular basis, such as monthly or even daily, after an account is opened. The purpose is to look for any situation where a customer is having trouble repaying other credit accounts or has taken on significantly higher levels of debt on those accounts.

In such a situation, the credit card issuer can unilaterally declare that you, the borrower, are in universal default and, if so, the default rate is applied to your account. Thus, under universal default, you can be charged a higher default rate on an account that you are handling just fine, simply because you are having trouble repaying another account. In fact, being late just once or twice on one account, such as a utility bill, car payment, or department store credit card, can trigger universal default on other accounts. The consumer's only recourse is to cancel the credit account.

Components of a Credit Score

FICO® scores are developed using complex statistical models that correlate certain borrower characteristics with the likelihood of repayment. The models are closely held secrets, but the factors that are used in the models are shared openly by Fair Isaac and Company on the company's web site:

1. **PAYMENT HISTORY** – Are you late with your payments? How late? How often? And on how many of your accounts?

2. **AMOUNTS OWED** – What is the balance on each of your credit obligations? How many accounts have balances? Are you "maxed out" or nearly so on your cards regardless of the dollar amount? Credit scores are negatively affected if you have a balance on any card in excess of thirty percent of the credit limit on that card.

3. **TAKING ON MORE DEBT?** – How many new accounts do you have? How long has it been since you opened a new account? How many recent inquiries have been made by lenders to whom you have made application? If you have had a period of poor credit usage in the past, for how long have you been in good standing?

4. **TYPES OF CREDIT USED** – Do you have a good mix of credit usage with reliance on multiple types depending on the purpose of the credit (for example, not using a credit card to buy a boat)? How many total accounts do you have?

5. **LENGTH OF CREDIT HISTORY** – How long have you had each account? How long has it been since you used the accounts?

Relative Weight of the Credit Score Components

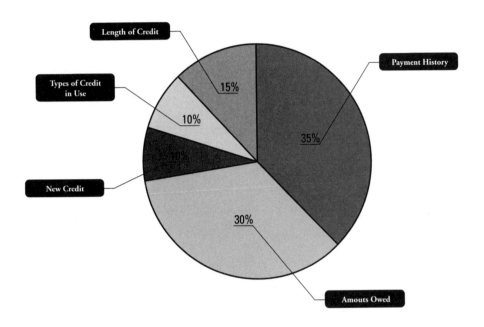

These percentages are based on the importance of the five categories for the general population. For particular groups—for example, people who have not been using credit long—the importance of some categories may be different.

FICO® Scoring Facts and Fallacies

FALLACY: **A poor score will haunt me forever.**

FACT: Just the opposite is true. A score is a "snapshot" of your risk at a particular point in time. It changes as new information is added to your bank and credit bureau files. Scores change gradually as you change the way you handle credit. For example, past credit problems impact your score less as time passes. Lenders request a current score when you apply for credit, so they have the most recent information available.

FALLACY: **Credit scoring is unfair to minorities.**

FACT: **Scoring does not consider your gender, race, nationality or marital status.** In fact, the Equal Credit Opportunity Act prohibits lenders from considering this type of information when issuing credit. Independent research has shown that credit scoring is not unfair to minorities or people with little credit history. Scoring has proven to be an accurate and consistent measure of repayment for all people who have some credit history. In other words, at a given score, non-minority and minority applicants are equally likely to pay as agreed.

FALLACY: **Credit scoring infringes on my privacy.**

FACT: **FICO® scores evaluate your credit report alone, which lenders already use to make credit decisions.** A score is simply a numeric summary of that information. In fact, lenders using scoring can often ask for less information about you. They may have fewer questions on the application form, for example.

FALLACY: **My score will drop if I apply for new credit.**

FACT: **Probably not much.** If you apply for several credit cards within a short period of time, multiple requests for your credit report information (called "inquiries") will appear on your report. Looking for new credit can equate with higher risk, but most credit scores are not affected by multiple inquiries from auto or mortgage lenders within a short period of time. The FICO® score treats these as a single inquiry, which will have less impact on your credit score.

What Information Affects Your FICO® Scores?

The answer to this question is both simple and complicated. It is simple because all the information in your credit histories at the national credit bureaus can affect your FICO® score. It is complicated because lots of different information can be in your credit file. Credit bureaus collect information from:

- Lenders
- Insurance Companies
- Landlords
- Public Utilities
- County Clerk's Offices
- The Courts
- Cellular Phone Companies.

Any of these sources might have provided information that sheds light on the five components of the credit score.

What Information Does Not Affect Your FICO® Scores

There are two categories of information that do not affect your credit score. The first is information that, by law, may not be used when evaluating a credit applicant. The Equal Credit Opportunity Acts prohibits use of the following types of information in credit scoring and other assessments of credit worthiness:

- Age
- Gender
- Marital Status
- Childbearing plans
- Location of Residence
- Race, national origin, ethnicity
- Source of income.

The second category of information that is not used to determine your credit score includes such factors as:

- Income stability and history
- Employment status and history
- Whether you own or rent
- Length of time at your current residence.

Note that lenders sometimes use each of these factors when evaluating applicants. They simply are not part of the credit scoring system. Thus, your credit score does not tell the whole story. Nonetheless, it is a vitally important part of your efforts to improve your credit status.

What You Can Do!

Action Module 6: Determining and Analyzing Your Credit Score

If you have been turned down for credit, the Equal Credit Opportunity Act (ECOA) gives you the right to obtain the reasons why within 30 days. You are also entitled to a free copy of your credit report within 60 days, which you can request from the credit reporting agencies.

If your credit score or something else in your credit report was a primary part of the lender's decision, the lender will use the score reason codes to explain to you why you didn't qualify for the requested credit. They often may not tell you your actual numerical score because the reasons for the score are more useful than the score itself, but you can still ask. If your application for credit was turned down or you didn't qualify for the interest rate you wanted, ask the lender how you can improve your credit picture.

Some lenders may tell you your credit score if they use it to make a lending decision. In California, state law requires lenders to tell you your score if they use it in connection with your mortgage application.

In reality, you should not wait until you are turned down for credit to find out your credit score. You should obtain your credit scores about six months before any major new application for credit, such as a car loan or home mortgage. This will allow you time to take action to address issues that may be negatively affecting your scores.

Under the Fair and Accurate Credit Transactions Act of 2003, consumers must be told their credit score. There usually is a nominal charge, between $5 and $7 for a credit score. You can contact all three of the three major credit bureaus by phone or on-line to obtain your credit scores. You will also be given the option to buy your credit score when you obtain free copies of your credit report at www.annualcreditreport.com. Consumers can also purchase credit reports and scores directly from the Credit Bureaus.

Equifax Inc.
1-800-685-1111
http://www.equifax.com

TransUnion™
1-800-888-4213
http://www.transunion.com

Experian®
1-888-243-6951
http://www.experian.com

Once you have your credit score from each of the national bureaus, you should match it up with your credit report obtained as discussed in Chapter 5. The following *Credit Score Summary Worksheet* can help you organize your information.

Action Module 6 | Credit Score Summary Worksheet

My Scores	Source of Credit Score		
	Experian®	Equifax	TransUnion™
My Scores	**Negative Factor Affecting My Score** (Put a mark in the box if reported on that particular credit report.)		
1. Payment History Factors			
Late payments on my credit accounts within the last two years			
Late payments for rent and utility bills within the last two years			
Charge-offs by lenders			
Bankruptcy in the last ten years			
Court judgments against me for debts or rent or utility bills			
2. Amount Owed Factors			
Overall amount owed is high for my income			
Balance on one or more credit card exceeds 30% of the credit limit			
A large number of accounts with balances			
3. New Additional Credit Factors			
Have been taking on considerable amounts of new credit			
A large number of inquiries from lenders in the last year			
Opened several credit card accounts in recent months			
4. Types of Credit in Use			
Many credit cards with some used irresponsibly			
Only one or two types of credit used			
High number of total accounts			
5. Length of Credit History			
Little or no usage of credit in the past			
All credit accounts are relatively new			
Some older accounts but a large number of accounts opened in recent months			

This worksheet is available for download at www.creditbooster.com/downloads/.

Do you have boxes with check marks? If so, there are aspects of your credit usage patterns that negatively affect your credit score. Some may be the result of errors or omissions in your credit bureau files. Others may be accurate and due to your credit behaviors in the past. In either case, there are actions you can take to improve your score. These will be addressed in *Section IV* of **CreditBooster**™ (particularly in Chapter 10).

Summary

- The information contained in your credit bureau files is used to calculate your credit score.

- FICO® scores are the most commonly used type of credit scores and each of the three major credit reporting agencies has its own version of a FICO® score.

- Your credit score will affect your ability to get credit and the interest you will pay for credit.

- There are five components of a FICO® score: payment history, amounts owed, your level of new debt, the types of credit you have used and how long you have been using credit.

- You should obtain your credit scores every year and, in conjunction with your credit reports, look for aspects of your credit history that may be negatively affecting your credit scores.

This section outlined how your financial/credit status is assessed in standard measures that others can use to determine whether or not to extend you additional credit. *Section IV: The Fix is On!* helps you begin the real work of taking the right steps necessary to improve your credit status. Here you will start taking the steps necessary to reduce your debt load and rebuild your credit reputation. Let's get started with *Chapter 7: Setting Your Financial Goals*, which helps you focus on setting financial goals that boost your credit status.

Chapter  7 | Setting Your Financial Goals

Section IV: The Fix is On! helps you begin the real work of taking the right steps necessary to improve your credit status. Here you will start taking the steps necessary to reduce your debt load and rebuild your credit reputation. This chapter helps you focus on setting financial goals that boost your credit status.

What You Need To Know!

The fact that you have completed the first six chapters shows that you have committed yourself to improving your credit status. Congratulations! This important goal is probably one of many of your financial goals. But having goals and reaching goals are two different things.

Experts in personal financial planning advise people to "pay themselves first." This means that the first dollars "spent" each week or month should actually be toward "saving" for identified goals.

Paying yourself first is part of what might be called the savings mentality. The savings mentality is the opposite of the credit mentality. You cannot succeed financially in life without developing a savings mentality. Savers win in life. Those who use credit too much do not achieve their financial goals. The credit mentality views borrowing as a primary way to reach goals. Nothing is further from the truth. Those who overuse credit "buy a fake lifestyle" based solely on credit, while savers create and live financially satisfying lives.

The savings mentality recognizes that:

- Saving is the only way to reach long-term financial goals.
- The only real way to get ahead is to spend less than you earn.

One nice thing about the savings mentality is that the more you focus on saving, the better your credit status and scores will become.

So! What do you do? You begin by setting financial goals. Then you set aside the money to get on the path to reach those goals. All good financial managers have in common setting goals and saving money to achieve them.

What Are Goals, and How Are They Different from Dreams?

A financial goal is something you intend to achieve. It is not a hope or just a dream. Dreams are vague. They start with "I wish." Financial goals are specific. They start with "I will." Goals are achieved by setting up a plan and then following that plan through to completion. When you get there you will be able to say "I am living my dream."

Consider the scenario of these two families: the Smiths and the Browns. The Smiths are dreamers. The Browns are planners.

The Smiths	The Browns
want to get out of debt.	will be out of debt.
would like to remodel their kitchen.	will remodel their kitchen.
think about retirement.	save for retirement.
hope eventually to send their child to college.	will have $10,000 saved for college tuition for their child.

Clearly, the Browns have started a strong game plan with a positive approach. If they work hard and follow their plan, there's a good chance they'll get what they're after.

The Smiths, on the other hand, have merely pointed out the things they wish for. Before they can set up a plan to realize their dreams, they will want to be much more positive and specific about their goals.

Your Values Provide the Basis for Your Goals

Your values are your fundamental beliefs about what is important, desirable, and worthwhile. They serve as the basis for your goals. All of us differ in the ways we value education, spiritual life, health, employment, credit use, family life, and many other factors.

Personal financial goals grow out of these values because we consider some things more important or desirable than others. We express our values, in part, by the ways we spend, save, and invest our money. It is clear that you value your credit reputation. That is why you are using **CreditBooster**™. Your goals should be consistent with your values.

To serve as a basis for financial actions, your goals must be stated explicitly. Financial goals should be specific both in terms of dollar amounts and the projected dates by which they are to be achieved. Setting goals helps you visualize the gap between your current financial status and where you want to be in the future.

General financial goals include finishing a college education, paying off debts (including education loans), taking a vacation, owning a home, accumulating funds to send children through college, owning your own business, and having financial independence at retirement. None of these goals, however, is specific enough to guide financial behavior. Specific goals should be measurable, attainable, relevant, and time-related.

How Do I Put Together a Set of Goals?

Goal setting is a step-by-step process. These steps are:

1. Identify your goals. You have completed that first step.
2. Set a deadline for achievement of the goal.
3. Estimate the total cost of the goal.
4. Estimate the monthly savings amount required.
5. Identify the ways you will reach the goal.
6. Take the first step.

Developing a goal chart is a good way to begin this process. Here's a sample Goal Chart that the Smiths have developed to turn three of their dreams into reality:

Sample Goal Chart				
Goal (specific)	Term (timely)	Total Cost (measurable)	Required Monthly Savings/Payment (realistic)	Ways to Reach (action-oriented)
To save for child's college	120 months	$20,000	$122	• Work one-day overtime per month. • Have funds automatically taken out of a checking account. • Put the money in a bond mutual fund each month.
Build a swimming pool	36 months	$12,000	$330	• Invest in mutual fund. • Do as much work on own. • Take a part-time job.
To remodel the kitchen	24 months	$5,000	$208	• Cut montly expenses by 5%. • Get a part-time job

You can start developing a goal chart of your own:

1. **Write one of your financial goals in the far left box of the chart below.**

Your Own Goal Chart				
Goal (specific)	Term (timely)	Total Cost (measurable)	Required Monthly Savings/Payment (realistic)	Ways to Reach (action-oriented)
Pay off a high credit card balance				

As you thought of which goal to write into the chart, you probably recognized that some of your goals are broad and far-reaching, while others may seem smaller in scope. It is okay to think big and for the long term, but be realistic about what you can attain. Because goals can vary so widely, it's a good idea to break them down into two separate categories of time:

*   Short-term goals generally take two years or less to achieve. Examples may include taking a vacation, buying a new refrigerator, or paying off a specific debt.

*   Long-term goals are those that can (or must) wait for more than two years. Examples might include college education for a child or a comfortable retirement.

2. **Let's add the time period to your goal. When would you like to have achieved your goal?**

Your Own Goal Chart				
Goal (specific)	Term (timely)	Total Cost (measurable)	Required Monthly Savings/Payment (realistic)	Ways to Reach (action-oriented)
Pay off a high credit card balance	*48 months*			

Next you will need to determine the total cost of your goal and determine the monthly savings amount needed.

It is easy to calculate the monthly savings amount needed for short-term goals. Simply divide the total amount needed by the number of months. In the example above, remodeling the Smiths' kitchen would require $208 ($5000/24) per month for 24 months.

Determining the dollar amounts for long-term goals is more complicated; but for goals to be achieved within five years, dividing the goal by the number of months is sufficiently accurate.

Because the goal of **CreditBooster**™ is to improve your credit status, one or more of your goals might be to pay off debts you owe. For loans you wish to pay off as originally agreed, you can use the regular monthly payment amount. For credit card debt and loans you wish to pay off early, you will need to calculate a monthly payment. You can visit the InCharge® Education Foundation Web site calculators at http://www.mindyourfinances.com/calculators to calculate the required amount.

3. **After completing your calculations, insert the total cost and required monthly savings amount for your goal in your chart.**

Your Own Goal Chart				
Goal (specific)	Term (timely)	Total Cost (measurable)	Required Monthly Savings/Payment (realistic)	Ways to Reach (action-oriented)
Pay off a high credit card balance	48 months	*$9,000*	*$250*	

4. **The final step in setting goals is to decide the actions you will take to achieve your goal. You can write in one or more ideas as you complete your chart.**

Your Own Goal Chart				
Goal (specific)	Term (timely)	Total Cost (measurable)	Required Monthly Savings/Payment (realistic)	Ways to Reach (action-oriented)
Pay off a high credit card balance	48 months	$9,000	$250	• *Cut back on meals out.* • *Drop premium cable channels.* • *Take a part-time job.*

So far you have focused on only one goal. You probably have others, as well. Later in this chapter you will complete a chart for all your major financial goals. But first, you need to give some thought to how you can prioritize your goals.

How Can I Prioritize My Goals?

We are keeping things pretty simple so far. You have only considered one goal. You might have as many as ten goals. Is it possible to achieve so many goals given your current situation? The answer is "probably not."

You will need to set priorities. Everyone has goals that cannot be achieved and others that must come first.

You might want to consider saving a little for multiple goals rather than putting all your effort into just one or two. Only you can decide on what goals are of the highest priority.

So, what should you do? You should get all your goals out on the table. Only when all your goals are identified can you set priorities. Setting priorities can be tough.

You may have goals related to retirement, paying off debts, buying a home, going on a vacation, buying a vehicle, and putting your children through college. You will need to select the most important from among all your goals.

Everyone has different values. Comparing yourself to others can get in the way of achieving what YOU really want. You may need to include family members in your thinking. But, you really need to think hard about what it is that you really want to achieve.

Here are some tips for setting priorities among your goals:

- **ADDRESS SHORT-TERM GOALS FIRST** – Reaching goals can be beneficial psychologically. Success breeds success. If goal setting is new to you or money is really tight, focus on a couple of easy short-term goals first. For example, you might focus on paying down debts and saving for the down payment on a new home.

- **DELAY FULLY FUNDING LONG-TERM GOALS** – Note that we did not say "delay funding long-term goals." The large dollar amounts needed for goals such as retirement, children's education, or saving for a home require saving for a long period of time. For example, a goal of having $100,000 in 20 years would require about $170 per month.

You might feel that it is impossible to save $170 per month. But waiting just five years to start increases the amount to $290 per month. You could however save $100 per month for five years and then $220 per month for the remaining 20 years. This pattern will also allow you to reach the $100,000 goal. Clearly, starting at some level is better than waiting to start at all.

- **USE AN OPPORTUNITY COST APPROACH** – An opportunity cost of a decision is what CANNOT be done if you go in a certain direction. For example, let's say you have three goals—to save for a vacation, to save for a down payment on a vehicle, and to get new carpeting. Knowing that you can't do all three, you might consider how you would feel if you chose the carpeting and giving up the vacation. If you needed to set aside $150 per month for a year to pay for the carpeting you would, of course, have the direct cost of the money set aside, but it would also carry the opportunity cost of delaying a desired vacation. Measuring both the direct and the opportunity cost of the carpeting lets you fully contemplate which of your goals should take priority.

Recognize where inappropriate priorities may have gotten you into trouble in the past. While not always true, many people trying to build (or rebuild their credit) recognize that they may have had their priorities misplaced. If this is you, you can take advantage of your fresh start to establish new priorities.

What You Can Do!

Action Module 7

The goal of **CreditBooster**™ is to help you improve your credit status. This general goal requires that you work on several specific goals that will change your financial status in ways that will make you more attractive to lenders.

One or more of your goals may involve paying off any debts you have; especially credit card debts where your balance exceeds 30% of your credit limit. That is because such balances have a negative affect on your credit score.

Another goal might be to establish a cash reserve equal to three months' worth of your household expense. This will improve your basic liquidity ratio and put money in the bank. Both of these factors are important to lenders.

And, of course, you will have other goals. Now is the time to put your thoughts into action. The **_Financial Goals Worksheet_** provides a way for you to get started. For best results, do not automatically assume a goal is unreachable. Go ahead and list any goal that you think is reasonably possible at some point in your life. After the worksheet is completed, you can set some priorities. But for now, think positively.

Action Module 7A | Financial Goals Worksheet

Your Own Goal Chart				
Goal (specific)	Term (timely)	Total Cost (measurable)	Required Monthly Savings/Payment (realistic)	Ways to Reach (action oriented)

This worksheet is available for download at www.creditbooster.com/downloads/.

You now have a list of goals. But it is probably painfully clear that you cannot begin to work on all of your goals right now. You need to set priorities. What should they be?

Because the purpose of **CreditBooster**™ is to help you improve your credit status, you will want to set a high priority on the goals that do just that. These will include any of your goals that reduce your current level of debt. Goals that build assets, especially monetary and investment assets, also will improve your credit status.

Less likely to improve your credit status are goals related to purchases or consumption such as buying furniture or taking a vacation. That is not to say that you should put a low priority on such goals. It is just that purchase goals have a small impact on your credit status. The one notable exception is the purchase of a home.

What are your top priority goals? Use the ***Goal Priority Worksheet*** to identify and record each of the top five. This may take some difficult thinking. Be sure to think of the opportunity cost aspects. When you put a high priority on a specific goal, it makes the achievement of some other goals less likely. Take care to recognize the opportunity costs of every goal you include in your priority list.

Action Module 7B │ Goal Priority Worksheet

Priority	Goal	Required Monthly Savings
#1		
#2		
#3		
#4		
#5		

This worksheet is available for download at www.creditbooster.com/downloads/.

Summary

- Goals are more than just dreams. They are more specific in terms of total dollar amounts needed, amounts to be set aside each month and target dates. They also include plans for how they might be achieved.

- Your goals should reflect your values. They are truly the things that are most important to you.

- Goals are both short- and long-term. Short-term goals are often interim steps toward completion of long-term goals

- Setting long-term goals requires that you factor in the effects of inflation and the interest you can earn off the funds being set aside. Calculators on the InCharge® Web site can help you make these calculations.

- You will likely not be able to start right away to achieve all your goals. You must set priorities for which goals you will work on first.

- Goals for paying down debts and building assets (rather than making purchases) will have the most impact on your credit status.

Identifying and prioritizing goals is a necessary part of improving your credit status. But the hard work has just begun. You will need to put into action the goals you have set for yourself.

The way to do put your goals into action is through budgeting. Remember the concept of "pay yourself first." The money needed to reach each goal you have chosen should be part of your budget and be the first amount you "spend" not the last. Chapter 8 will cover budgeting.

In Chapter 7 you established specific goals. Here in Chapter 8, you will develop a plan. But not just any plan. You will develop a Spending Plan that includes provisions for reaching your goals. For that is the real purpose of planning—the achievement of financial goals.

What You Need To Know!

Getting a handle on your finances is a three-step process. First, you need to know where you stand in *the present*. This step was covered in Chapter 2. Second, you need look back to assess your finances in *the past*. This step was covered in Chapter 3. Third, you need to plan what you want to do in *the future* to improve your finances. This third step requires that you set up a Spending Plan which is commonly referred to as a "budget."

Budgets tend to be very restrictive and hard to live with over time. Your Spending Plan will be a plan for your financial behavior so you can get ahead rather than fall further and further behind. A Spending Plan is not a strict "diet" where you record every dollar spent; rather it is a guide for future spending.

Planning gives you control over your spending so you can reach your goals and prepare for unforeseen events that otherwise set you back.

A Spending Plan is simply a plan designed to balance income and spending while achieving financial goals.

A Spending Plan can help you:

- Avoid overspending
- Save money
- Establish financial control and direction
- Prepare for emergencies and unexpected events
- Achieve your goals.

Each of these benefits of planning will enhance your credit status.

The key to financial success is spending less than you earn. That means saving. Saving should be something you do on a regular basis. An important philosophy in personal financial planning is to "pay yourself first." This means that saving is planned and occurs at the beginning of the month—not at the end of the month. If you wait to see how much money will be left over, you are likely to find that nothing is left over. If you have saved at the beginning of a month and also find at the end of the month that you have some money left over, consider putting those dollars into savings as well. Your credit status will improve considerably if you have money saved in bank accounts, retirement accounts, and other places.

Planning Your Income!

When people think of financial planning, most think only of planning their spending, but income can be planned and projected as well. It may be easy to predict your income if you have a fixed monthly salary. But many people's income will vary from month to month. One way to predict income is to look back at what happened during the previous months. Often, you will be able to see seasonal patterns. Perhaps you tend to work overtime in July and August. You can then factor that pattern into your budgets for those months.

You can use **Worksheet 8A: Planned Income** to record your planned income for the next month.

In order to complete the worksheet, you will need to go back over your records. Refer back to **Worksheet 3A: Income** in Chapter 3 and project what changes might occur in your income for the next month. Perhaps ask family members, too. Then write those figures in the "**$ Amount**" column. Adding all the amounts reveals "**Total Income.**"

Next, you will also find it helpful to calculate the percentage of your income that comes from the various sources. Once you add up all your income, that amount equals 100%. To calculate each income amount as a percentage, you divide each income item by total income and multiply it by 100.

For example, if your total income is $3000 per month and gross salary (before taxes and other withholdings) in "Gross Salary #1" is $2700, divide the $2700 by $3000. Now you know that 90% ($2700/$3000 x 100) of your total income comes from that source.

Worksheet 8A | My Next Month's Planned Income

Income	$ Amount	% of Total Income
Gross Salary #1		
Gross Salary #2		
Social Security Benefits #1		
Social Security Benefits #2		
Interest Income		
Annunity Income		
Pension Benefits		
Dividend Income		
Gifts		
Other Income		
TOTAL INCOME		

This worksheet is available for download at www.creditbooster.com/downloads/.

Planning Your Spending!

Planning your spending is the next step. Everyone's Plan is and should be different. There is no right or wrong to the amounts you decide to spend for various purposes.

The next two worksheets will help you budget your spending for the next month. You can start by referring to the information on your expenses that you gathered in Chapter 3. You also now have some new goals developed in Chapter 5. The amounts needed for these goals are summarized in *Action Module 7B*. You will want to include these amounts in your Plan as well. As in Chapter 3, you will divide your expenses into two groups: fixed and variable expenses.

Planned Fixed Expenses

Worksheet 8B: My Next Month's Planned Fixed Expenses can be used to list your fixed expense amounts for the next month. *Worksheet 3-B: Fixed Expenses* from Chapter 3 will give you a starting point for deciding on spending in each category the next month. The worksheet below has one big change from the one used in Chapter 3. Five new categories have been added to reflect your five new goals. These are included in fixed expenses in keeping with the philosophy of "pay yourself first." Again, you should write in the amount for each fixed expense item and add them up to obtain your total fixed expenses. Then, to calculate each fixed expense amount as a percentage of your income, you divide each item by total income (not total fixed expenses) and multiply it by 100.

For example, if your rent payment is $900 per month and total income is $3000, divide the $900 by $3000. Now you know that 30% ($900/$3000 x 100) of your total income is used to pay your rent.

Worksheet 8B | My Next Month's Planned Fixed Expenses

Fixed Expenses	$ Amount	% of Total Income
Fixed Savings		
Rent or Mortgage Payment		
Homeowner's Insurance *(if not in mortgage)*		
Property Taxes		
Auto Insurance Car #1		
Auto Insurance – Car #2		
Life insurance		
Health Insurance		
Other Insurance		
Federal Income Taxes		

(continued)

(continued)

Fixed Expenses	$ Amount	% of Total Income
Social Security Taxes		
State Income Taxes		
Local Income Taxes		
Internet Access		
Cell Phone #1 Base Charge		
Cell Phone #2 Base Charge		
Donations		
Loan Payment #1		
Loan Payment #2		
Loan Payment #3		
Loan Payment #4		
Monthly Allocation to Goal #1		
Monthly Allocation to Goal # 2		
Monthly Allocation to Goal # 3		
Monthly Allocation to Goal # 4		
Monthly Allocation to Goal # 5		
Other Fixed Expenses		
TOTAL FIXED EXPENSES		

This worksheet is available for download at www.creditbooster.com/downloads/.

Planned Variable Expenses

Worksheet 8C: My Next Month's Planned Variable Expenses can be used to list your variable expenses. Again, you should write in the amount for each variable expense item and add them up to obtain your total variable expenses. Then, to calculate each variable expense amount as a percentage of your income, you divide each item by total income (not total variable expenses) and multiply it by 100.

For example, if your Food (at home) expense is $600 per month and gross salary (before taxes and other withholdings) in "Gross Salary #1" is $3000, divide the $600 by $3000. Now you know that 20% ($600/$3000 x 100) of your total income is goes toward food consumed at home.

Worksheet 8C | My Next Month's Planned Variable Expenses

Variable Expenses	$ Amount	% of Total Income
Variable Savings		
Food (at home)		
Food (away from home)		
Utilities		
Cell Phone Extra Minutes		
Cell Phone Roaming Fees		
Household Operations		
Gasoline, Oil Vehicle Maintence		
Medical Expenses		
Medicines		
Clothing and Upkeep		
Credit Card Payment #1		
Credit Card Payment #2		

(continued)

(continued)

Variable Expenses	$ Amount	% of Total Income
Credit Card Payment #3		
Credit Card Payment #4		
Entertainment		
Gifts		
Personal Allowances		
Personal Care		
Charitable Contributions		
Miscellaneous		
Other Variable Expenses		
TOTAL VARIABLE EXPENSES		

This worksheet is available for download at www.creditbooster.com/downloads/

What You Can Do!

Action Module 8

The three worksheets tell you what you plan as income and spending for the upcoming month.

Your work is not quite complete until you take the time to analyze your planned income and expenses and calculate whether you will break even (your expenses equal income), have a deficit (expenses exceed income); or, the best case scenario, you will enjoy a surplus where your income actually exceeds your expenses.

The greater your income in relation to your expenses, the greater the control over your family's personal finances and more financial opportunities will become available to you.

Balancing Your Spending Plan!

Now comes the moment of truth:

Enter your Total Income (from *Worksheet 8A*) . . . . _____(1)

Add your Total Fixed Expenses (from *Worksheet 8B*) . . . . + _____

to your Total Variable Expenses (from *Worksheet 8C*) . . . . _____

= _____(2)

From (1) _____

Subtract (2) _____

Your Projected Surplus (or Deficit) . . . . = _____

Did you plan to spend less than your income? You have a surplus. If so, you can make changes in your spending to reflect the surplus. Or, even better, you could allocate the surplus to saving for one or more of your goals, to an emergency savings fund, or to a variable savings account.

Or did you plan to spend more than your income? You have a deficit. If so, you will need to make some changes in spending and income categories to bring your budget into balance. In Chapter 3, you made preliminary lists of ways you could increase income and decrease spending (*Action Module 3*). You can refer back to those lists as you think of ways to bring your budget into balance.

Action Module 8: Your Final Spending Plan

Once you have adjusted your worksheets to bring your Plan into balance you can set up your final Spending Plan:

My Spending Plan for _____ month/year

Action Module 8 | Your Final Spending Plan

Income	Dollars	%
Gross Salary #1		
Gross Salary #2		
Gross Salary #3		
Social Security Benefits #1		
Social Security Benefits #2		
Interest Income		
Annuity Income		
Pension Benefits		
Dividend Income		
Gifts		
Other Income		
TOTAL INCOME		
Expenses	**Dollars**	**%**
Fixed Savings		
Rent or Mortgage Payment		
Homeowner's Insurance *(if not in mortgage)*		
Automobile Insurance - Car #1		
Automobile Insurance - Car # 2		
Life Insurance		
Health Insurance		
Other Insurance		

(continued)

(continued)

Fixed Expenses	Dollars	%
Federal Income Taxes		
State Income Taxes		
Social Security Taxes		
Local Income Taxes		
Personal Property Taxes		
Internet Access		
Cell Phone #1 Base Charges		
Cell Phone #2 Base Charges		
Donations		
Loan Payment #1		
Loan Payment #2		
Loan Payment #3		
Loan Payment #4		
Monthly Allocation to Goal #1		
Monthly Allocation to Goal #2		
Monthly Allocation to Goal #3		
Monthly Allocation to Goal #4		
Other Fixed Expenses		
TOTAL FIXED EXPENSES		
Variable Expenses	Dollars	%
Variable Savings		
Food (at home)		
Food (away from home)		

(continued)

(continued)

Variable Expenses	Dollars	%
Clothing and Upkeep		
Utilities		
Cell Phone Additional Fees		
Household Operations		
Gasoline, Oil, Vehicle Maintenance		
Medical Expenses		
Medicines		
Credit Card Payment #1		
Credit Card Payment #2		
Credit Card Payment #3		
Credit Card Payment #4		
Entertainment		
Gifts		
Personal Allowances		
Personal Care		
Charitable Contributions		
Miscellaneous		
Other Variable Expenses		
TOTAL VARIABLE EXPENSES		
TOTAL EXPENSES		
Net Surplus (or Deficit) **TOTAL INCOME** **– TOTAL EXPENSES**	=	

This worksheet is available for download at www.creditbooster.com/downloads/.

Living Your Plan!

Planning income and expenses is the initial step. Once the month begins, the Plan then helps you control your spending during the month. There are several spending controls to help you stay on target. Here are four spending controls that work:

1. **USE A CHECKING ACCOUNT** – People who use cash frequently have trouble tracking the amount they spend. In contrast, checks provide a record of each transaction. The check contains a space to record the purpose. It is also a good control measure to deposit all income directly into your checking account. Then, if you need cash, write a check and note on it and in the check register why you needed the cash.

   Take special care if you use automatic teller machines frequently to withdraw cash or use debit cards to pay for things. These transactions should be recorded in the check register immediately. Also record the budget expenditure category for which the funds were used.

2. **USE A NOTEBOOK** – Recall from Chapter 3 that we recommended using a notebook to keep track of spending. The notebook can be also be used to keep your spending under control. Example 8.1 shows a notebook page for the spending category of "Food Away from Home". In our example, there is a budget of $140 for the month. A notebook page is set based on the planned amount. Then as money is spent in that category, it is subtracted from the amount remaining to be spent. At any point during the month you will know exactly where you stand. For example, in this case, no more spending will be allowed in this category after July 21.

Example 8.1 | Spending Plan Notebook Page

Category: FOOD AWAY FROM HOME	Amount Spent	July Planned Amount Remaining to Spend
July 3 - Fast food dinner before concert	$17	$83
July 10 - Lunch with friends	$18	$63
July 15 - Birthday dinner for Jim	$44	$17
July 21 - Sunday brunch after church	$17	$0

3. **USE THE ENVELOPE SYSTEM** – The envelope system works well for budget expense categories where cash is used. Here is how it works:

- At the start of a budgeting period, place the budgeted amount of money into an envelope for each category.

- Write the classification name and the budget amount on the outside of each envelope.

- As expenditures are made, record them on the appropriate envelope and remove the proper amounts of cash.

- When an envelope is empty, funds are exhausted for that classification.

This technique works well in controlling expenditures for variable expenses such as entertainment, personal allowances, and food. It may also provide a good way for younger children to learn to budget their allowances. Be sure to keep the envelopes in a safe place.

4. **USE ALLOWANCES** – Keeping track of every dollar can be tough. This is especially true for small day-to-day spending on snacks, personal items, coffee, and similar expenses. Each family member could receive a weekly or monthly allowance for such items. That way it is not necessary to record every item; just record the allowance amount as paid. If one runs out of allowance money, that person has to wait until the beginning of the next month for a new allowance amount.

How Do You Know If Your Planning Was Successful?

Evaluation is the final step in the Spending Plan process. Evaluation tells you whether the earlier steps in the planning process have worked. During the evaluation you should:

- Compare actual income and spending with budgeted amounts
- Decide how to handle any left over balances
- Judge your success in reaching your goals
- Get ready for the next budget cycle.

COMPARE PLANNED AND ACTUAL AMOUNTS – Comparing your planned and actual income and spending amounts is vitally important. Sometimes called variance analysis, it involves looking at each spending category to see if you met your targets. The idea is to determine if the expense "varied" from what was planned. Was it different from the planned amount? In some Plan expenditure classifications, the planned estimates rarely agree with the actual expenditures—particularly in variable expenses.

Missing a few targets may cause little concern. However, if excessive variances have prevented you from achieving your objectives or making the Plan balance, then you will need to take stronger action to control spending.

At the end of the planned time period, some classifications—especially variable expenses— may still have a positive balance. For example, perhaps you estimated the electric bill at $50, and it was only $45. What should you do? For small overages, you might allocate that extra amount into the same category for the following month, thereby providing a larger estimate for the next time period.

Because variable expense estimates are usually averages, it is best not to change the estimate based on a variance that occurs over just one or two months. If estimates are too high or low for a longer period, however, you will want to make adjustments.

DEAL WITH LEFT-OVER BALANCES –One of the most frequent questions is what to do with a balance left over in a certain category. The excess may look like "found money" that is mighty tempting for use on some unplanned item.

Assume, for example, you budgeted $60 per month for car insurance. But the bill comes in every six months. In all the other months it looks as if you have money left over at the end of the month. But you will need that money later. You should move it into a savings account (perhaps one opened just for that purpose) to await the arrival of the insurance bill.

ASSESS PROGRESS TOWARD GOALS – Whatever your goals, it is satisfying to know that you have made progress towards reaching them. Staying within planned estimates, reducing the amount owed on a loan, paying off a small debt, or saving $20 during a budget period allows you to say, "I did it! I succeeded because I made a plan and implemented it successfully. "

GET READY FOR THE NEXT BUDGET CYCLE – If you did not achieve some of your objectives, you can use the evaluation process to determine why. Then you can adjust your next month's budget and objectives accordingly. Maybe you had unexpected medical expenses or an out-of-town trip to visit a sick relative. Under these circumstances, you can easily understand why the objective was not achieved. Then you can set your sights on reaching your budgeting goals during the next budgeting time period.

Evaluation of your progress toward reaching savings goals is very important. As seen in Chapter 3, net worth can grow only when you spend less than your income. Financial success comes when savings goals are being met. If this is not the case for you, the budgeter—you—must set up mechanisms to force savings to occur. Payroll deductions and automatic transfers from checking to savings accounts, for example, may aid this process by making saving automatic. Such techniques are especially useful for people new to the process of budgeting.

Summary

- A Spending Plan is a plan for income and spending designed to balance the two while achieving financial goals.

- Once you have estimated your planned income and spending for the month, you will probably have to go back and adjust one or more categories so that your Plan will balance.

- Spending controls help you stay on target during the month. Four particularly effective spending controls are your checkbook, using a spending notebook, the envelope method, and allowances.

- Evaluation at the end of the month is the final step in planning. It is important in this step to look at each income and expense category that varied from what was planned, so that subsequent months can be adjusted accordingly. If you have money left over in some categories that you know you will need to spend in later months, you should transfer those funds into a savings account so they will be available when needed.

Section IV: The Fix is On! helps you begin the real work of taking the right steps necessary to improve your credit status. This chapter helped you develop a Spending Plan that will help you reach the financial goals you formed in Chapter 7. *Chapter 9: Removing Mistakes from Your Credit Report* provides you assistance and advice in spotlighting errors and omissions in your credit reports and correcting those mistakes.

In Chapter 7 you established specific goals. In Chapter 8, you developed a Spending Plan, including provisions for reaching your goals. Both of these tasks will improve your financial condition and, as a result, your standing in the eyes of creditors. In this chapter you will focus on removing mistakes from your credit report.

What You Need To Know!

At first glance, looking at a credit report can be a bit overwhelming or intimidating, because there are lots of details. But you have already learned how to read your credit report. Now, by applying the steps in this chapter, you can remove any mistakes and add any good information that should be in your credit report.

Why You Should Fix Mistakes in Your Credit Report

If your credit report contains errors, it could affect your credit rating, resulting in increased interest rates or even denial of credit. Getting errors fixed on your credit report is not particularly difficult, but it can take several months. So it is important that you review your credit report well before you plan to take out a loan and make it a habit to review it at least once a year. In Chapter 5 you learned how to check your report and request the three major national credit bureaus to send you your reports.

If you have problems understanding anything in your credit report, telephone the credit bureau and request an explanation. Credit bureaus are required by law to explain information in your report that you don't understand. Be aware, though, that sometimes it may take awhile to get an answer to your question when you call. You might try calling during off-peak hours for faster service, such as before 8 a.m. and after 10 p.m. Credit bureaus also are required to explain what an entry means, but not why an entry exists on your credit report.

Each of the national bureaus has toll-free telephone access. Visiting their web sites may result in a faster response.

Equifax Inc. 1-800-685-1111
http://www.equifax.com/dispute

Experian® 1-888-397-3742
http://www.experian.com/disputes

TransUnion™ 1-800-916-8800
http://www.transunion.com/corporate/personal/creditDisputes.page

The credit bureau web sites also contain good explanations, so look there, too, especially at the "FAQs" section, "Frequently Asked Questions."

Removing Errors from Your Credit Report

In Chapter 5 you requested your credit reports and you carefully analyzed each of them for errors, any missing good credit history information, and other entries that would set off warning bells to potential creditors. You then completed *Action Module 5*, where you listed all of the erroneous information in your reports. You might want to go over your reports again to make sure you have found all the errors. Let's review again the types of errors that can occur in credit reports:

MISSING ACCOUNTS

- Credit accounts that you have but that are missing from your reports.

CORRECTING PERSONAL DATA ERRORS

- Incorrect names, addresses, telephone numbers, or Social Security numbers on accounts.

CORRECTING ERRORS IN YOUR LISTED ACCOUNTS

- Accounts that are not yours.
- Lawsuits or public actions in which you are not involved.
- Incorrect account histories (saying you were late when you actually made payments on time).
- Accounts listed as a "chargeoff" (debt that was written off and never paid) that you actually did pay in full.
- Accounts that you have closed or paid off but are still listed as active.
- Accounts that should be the responsibility of a divorced spouse.

The **Federal Fair Credit Reporting Act (FCRA)** requires that credit reports be accurate. It also provides a way for consumers to have errors removed or corrected. If you found any error or omissions in your reports, you should take immediate steps to get the information corrected. You can dispute errors by mail or on-line. Contact information is provided below in *Action Module 9*.

We present below, for each type of credit report error, steps that you can take to get the information corrected. Included here are sample letters you can use to challenge and correct errors. The information we have included also would be needed should you choose to use the on-line method instead of writing a letter. To save time, you should gather the relevant information and have it available when you begin your on-line challenges and corrections of errors.

Downloadable copies of these letters are available at no cost at www.creditbooster.com.

Correcting Missing Account Errors

Credit reports sometimes fail to include all of your accounts. You certainly would want to make sure all missing accounts for which you have good credit history are included in your report. In such cases, you are not asking for reaffirmation but simply notifying the credit bureau of the accounts and asking that they be included in your file. Here is a sample letter from Jane Doe requesting that a missing account be added to her file:

Sample Letter Asking that Account Information Be Added to Your Account

---

June 5, 20XX

Experian
P.O. Box 2104
Allen TX, 75013-2104

Dear Sir or Madam:

I have discovered the following missing items in my credit report. With this letter, I assert my rights under the Fair Credit Reporting Act (FCRA) to have these items included in my report. Please take steps to have this item added to my file.

JetAway Oil Company Credit Card, opened July, 2002.
Account number: 1234-5678-9101-1121.
Account address: 1234 Main Street, Anytown, TX 76147.
Account holder: Jane Doe.

Best regards,

Jane Doe

Jane should also write a letter to JetAway Oil Company to request that her account information be sent to the national credit bureaus.

Correcting Personal Data Errors

Credit bureaus sometimes have incorrect personal information in your files. Most common of these types of errors are mailing address and telephone numbers as these change from time to time. To correct missing personal data, send a letter to the credit bureau requesting that it be updated to reflect the new personal data you are providing. The following page contains a sample letter by Jane Doe requesting correction of her current mailing address. Note the additional identifying information in the letter. This will make it clear to the bureau that the request is actually coming from Jane.

Sample Letter Asking for Correction of Personal Information

June 5, 20xx

Experian
P.O. Box 2104
Allen TX, 75013-2104

Dear Sir or Madam:

I have discovered the following errors in my credit report related to my personal information.

My mailing address is wrong.

My current address is:
1234 Main St., Anytown, TX 76147

My full name is Jane Ann Doe

Date of birth: June 1, 1951
SSN: 123-45-6789,
Phone number: 615-555-5555.

My previous addresses are:
-1724 West Elm Street, Anytown, TN 37220
-114 Shakespeare Ct, Metropolis, NY 11032

Best regards,

Jane Doe

Correcting Errors in Your Listed Accounts

The most serious type of credit bureau error involves reports about accounts that are not yours or that show erroneous account histories such as being past due when the account is really in good standing. The FCRA outlines the specific steps you should take to challenge such errors. Notify the bureau, in writing, that you wish to exercise your right to a reaffirmation of an item under the FCRA. Specifically, you should ask the bureau to "reaffirm" the item. To reaffirm means to validate that the information is correct. If the credit bureau cannot do so within 30 days, the law requires that the item be removed.

The following page contains a sample letter requesting reaffirmation of two entries in Jane Doe's credit bureau file. Again, note the additional identifying information in the letter. This will make it clear to the bureau that the request is actually coming from Jane.

Sample Letter Asking for Reaffirmation of An Error

June 5, 20XX

Experian
P.O. Box 2104
Allen TX, 75013-2104

Dear Sir or Madam:

I have discovered the following errors in my credit report. With this letter, I assert my rights under the Fair Credit Reporting Act (FCRA) to have these items reaffirmed. Please takes steps to reaffirm these items. If they cannot be reaffirmed, please remove them from my record.

If they are affirmed, I will be asserting my rights under the FCRA to challenge the items that I dispute.

Here are the items I believe are errors:

Lein filed 3/99, Newark, NJ case number 73654
This is not mine. I have never lived in or done business with anyone in New Jersey.

Account past due, case number 67543. "Togs for Tots" store account
This account is current and has no outstanding balance at this time.

My full name is Jane Ann Doe
Date of birth: June 1, 1951
SSN: 123-45-6789
Phone number: 615-555-5555.

My previous addresses are:
-1724 West Elm Street, Anytown, TN 37220
-114 Shakespeare Ct, Metropolis, NY 11032

My current address is: 1234 Main St., Anytown, TX 76147

Best regards,

Jane Doe

As credit bureaus get their information from creditors it is highly likely that the creditor will simply report back that the information is correct. Nonetheless, asking for reaffirmation is the first step for you to challenge an error. Your reaffirmation can often clear up a problem, especially if the credit bureau and not the creditor made the error. If the credit bureau responds saying that the information is accurate, you then have the right to challenge the accuracy of the item formally with both the credit bureau and the creditor involved. Within 30 days, the credit bureau must reinvestigate the information that you challenge. If the bureau cannot complete its investigation within 30 days, it must drop the information from your credit file.

For example, Jane Doe was told by the credit bureau that the account with the erroneously reported lien was indeed an error and would be removed. However, the bureau maintained that the past due account was affirmed by the creditor and would not be removed.

Jane should send letters to both the bureau and the creditor. Her credit report will have the contact information for the creditor, or she can check for the address to use on her most recent billing statement. The following page contains Jane's letters formally challenging the (A) credit bureau and the (B) creditor on past due account information.

(A) Sample Letter to the Credit Bureau Challenging an Error

June 5, 20XX

Experian
P.O. Box 2104
Allen TX, 75013-2104

Dear Sir or Madam:

I have enclosed a photocopy of your recent letter stating that the creditor has reaffirmed the error described below. With this letter, Assert my rights under the Fair Credit Reporting Act (FCRA) to challenge this error formally. Please take steps to reinvestigate this item.

> ***Account past due, case number 67543. "Togs for Tots" store account***
> *This account is current and has no outstanding balance at this time. Please remove the "past due" statement from this account. Attached you will find a photocopy of my most recent billing statement showing a $0 balance on the account.*

My full name is Jane Ann Doe, date of birth June 1, 1951, SSN 123-45-6789, phone number 615-555-5555.

My previous addresses are:
>   *-1724 West Elm Street, Anytown, TN 37220*
>   *-114 Shakespeare Ct, Metropolis, NY 11032*

My current address is: 1234 Main St., Anytown, TX 76147

Best regards,

Jane Doe

B) Sample Letter to The Creditor Challenging an Error

June 5, 2004

Togs for Tots
P.O. Box 6789
Lexington, KY 40519-6789

Dear Sir or Madam,

I have enclosed a recent letter from the Experian Credit Bureau stating that the error below was reaffirmed.

With this letter, I assert my rights under the Fair Credit Reporting Act (FCRA) to challenge this error formally. Please take steps to reinvestigate this item.

> **Account past due, case number 67543. "Togs for Tots" store account**
> *This account is current and has no outstanding balance at this time. Please remove the "past due" statement from this account AND NOTIFY EXPERIAN OF THIS CORRECTION. Attached you will find a photocopy of my most recent billing statement showing a $0 balance on the account.*

My full name is Jane Ann Doe, date of birth June 1, 1951, SSN 123-45-6789, phone number 615-555-5555.

My previous addresses are:
*   -1724 West Elm Street, Anytown, TN 37220*
*   -114 Shakespeare Ct, Metropolis, NY 11032*

My current address is: 1234 Main St., Anytown, TX 76147

Best regards,

Jane Doe

If the information is an error, it must be corrected. Plus, if a report containing the error had been sent by a credit bureau to a creditor during the past six months, a corrected report must be sent to that creditor. To remove an error in your credit report, send a letter to the credit bureau that clearly explains the error. Include a photocopy (not the original) of any supporting documentation. If you do not hear from the credit bureau in 30 days, send the same letter again along with a photocopy of your first letter.

What to Do if the Mistake Is Not Removed

If the credit bureau and the creditor do not agree with you and will not remove the disputed entry, the FCRA allows you to insert a 100-word consumer statement into your credit bureau file describing your side of the dispute. You should send a letter and the statement to the credit bureau asking that the statement be added to your credit report. Credit bureaus are required to attach your consumer statement to your credit report, so you can always give your side of the story.

Here is an example of a consumer statement Jane Doe might write if the bureau and creditor will not remove the erroneous information about a past-due account.

Sample Consumer Statement Submitted to Credit Bureau

June 5, 20XX

Experian
P.O. Box 2104
Allen TX, 75013-2104

Dear Sir or Madam:

I am enclosing the following Consumer Statement to be include in my credit report:

The information from Togs for Tots that states that my account is past due is not correct. I have paid the account on time every month since opening the account in November, 1999. I have a copy of my most recent monthly statement showing that the balance owed is $0."

My full name is Jane Ann Doe, date of birth June 1, 1951, SSN 123-45-6789, phone number 615-555-5555.

My previous addresses are:
 -1724 West Elm Street, Anytown, TN 37220
 -114 Shakespeare Ct, Metropolis, NY 11032

My current address is: 1234 Main St., Anytown, TX 76147

Best regards,

Jane Doe

What You Can Do!

Action Module 9: Correcting Credit Report Errors

Now It's Your Turn! Are there errors in your credit reports? If so, you will want to have them corrected as soon as possible. Look back to **Action Module 5** in Chapter 5 where you recorded the errors you found in your reports.

Here are the dispute addresses for each of the three major credit bureaus:

Experian®
Use the address listed on your credit report.

TransUnion™ Consumer Solutions
P.O. Box 2000
Chester, PA 19022-2000

Equifax Information Services, LLC
P.O. Box 740256
Atlanta, GA 30374

Visiting their web sites may result in a faster response.

Experian®
http://www.experian.com/disputes

TransUnion™ Consumer Solutions
http://www.transunion.com/corporate/personal/creditDisputes.page

Equifax Information Services, LLC
http://www.equifax.com/dispute then click on "online dispute"

Experian® and the Experian® marks herein are service marks or registered trademarks of Experian®, Inc. Equifax and the Equifax marks herein are service marks or registered trademarks of Equifax, Inc. TransUnion™ and the TransUnion™ marks herein are service marks or registered trademarks of TransUnion™, LLC.

You also will need to determine the mailing addresses for your creditors. Look at recent bills for that information.

Action Module 9A | Mailing Address of Credit Bureaus and Creditors for Your Disputed Items

Nature of Dispute	Name and Address of Credit Bureau	Name and Address of Creditor
#1		
#2		
#3		
#4		
#5		

This worksheet is available for download at www.creditbooster.com/downloads/

Sample Consumer Statement Submitted to Credit Bureau

The table below will help you keep track of your progress while you are disputing errors in your credit reports. You should record each step in the process as your files are corrected.

Action Module 9B | Credit Report Dispute Tracking Worksheet

Step	File Case 1	File Case 2	File Case 3	File Case 4	File Case 5
Credit Bureau Reporting the Error					
Creditor Name					
Nature of the Error					
Date Initial Reaffirmation Letter Sent to the Bureau					
Date and Nature of Response Received					
Date Letter of Challenge Sent to the Bureau					
Date and Nature of Response Received					
Date Letter of Challenge Sent to the Creditor					
Date and Nature of Response Received					
Date Consumer Statement Sent to Credit Bureau					

This worksheet is available for download at www.creditbooster com/downloads/.

Summary

- There are three basic types of errors: 1) missing accounts, 2) errors related to your personal history such as your current address, and 3) errors in your listed accounts.

- To add missing accounts, contact the credit bureau and the creditor and ask that your credit history be updated to show the missing account.

- To remove an error in your credit report, send a letter to the credit bureau that clearly explains the error and includes supporting documentation.

- If the credit bureau doesn't agree with you and will not remove a disputed entry, you may send a 100-word consumer statement along with a cover letter to the credit bureau asking that the statement be added to your credit report.

Section IV: The Fix is On! helps you begin the real work of taking the right steps necessary to improve your credit status. This chapter provides you assistance and advice in removing mistakes from your credit report that you spotlighted in Chapter 5. Chapter 10 will focus on improving your credit scores and provide you with information on how you can do even more to improve your credit status.

Chapter 9 provided you assistance and advice in removing mistakes from your credit report that you spotlighted in Chapter 5. Chapter 10 will focus on improving your credit scores and provide you with information on how you can do even more to improve your credit status. Doing so will go a long way towards improving your credit score because your credit score is derived from the information in your credit report. But there is even more you can do. This chapter covers techniques for raising your credit score as high as possible. The benefits will be two-fold—you will have greater access to credit and the credit you obtain will cost less.

What You Need To Know!

You may find that your credit score is still lower than you would like (or deserve) even after making sure your credit report is accurate. The average FICO® credit score has fluctuated between 675 and 700 in recent years, with 850 being the maximum score one could have. As you saw in Chapter 6, people with below-average scores must pay high interest rates.

What can you do?

First, you need to recognize that efforts to improve your credit score take time to have an impact. Most people find that it takes about one year for their score to show much improvement. This is partly because changes take time to show up in your credit report.

It is also true that your credit history stays with you for a long time. If your history is positive, that is a real plus. But if your history has some negatives, those stay in your credit file for seven years. New positive information helps, but it does not erase old negative information.

Nonetheless, waiting to do something about a low score only prolongs the problem. The time to get started is now. Basically, there are two broad categories for the things you can do to improve your credit score. The first involves improving your financial behaviors. The second involves changing your debt situation. For each, let's list things you should DO and things you should *NOT DO*.

Improving Your Financial Behaviors

DO pay your bills on time. The largest single component of a credit score is your payment history. If you are late on or skip payments on items such as credit cards or vehicle loans, your score will surely be affected. This is true for installment debt payments—such as a television—and any of your monthly bills, such as your utilities. This is because many merchants—not just lenders—report payment patterns to credit bureaus.

DO focus any search to obtain new credit within a short period of time, such as one month. The number of inquiries from lenders in your credit bureau file negatively affects your credit score. If the inquiries all come in within thirty days they will all be recognized as part of one search—such as for an auto loan. But if you spread your search over several months the pattern will look like multiple searches—a negative in most credit scoring systems.

DO check your credit score periodically—perhaps every six months while you are working to rebuild your credit score. Your own inquiries do not negatively impact your credit score. Make sure you get your score directly from the credit bureaus or from FICO®. Using a second party to get the score (such as the many "free offers" you might see on the Internet) will be viewed as coming from a lender. This means they will be counted as a lender inquiry, and that is a negative.

DO avoid applying for any new credit for one year. Inquiries from creditors are automatically deleted from your record after twelve months. This technique is especially helpful if your credit report currently shows a high number of inquiries. That fact, in and of itself, may be the major reason for a lower than necessary credit score.

DO NOT ignore bills for which you are currently behind. Bring them up-to-date.

DO NOT open multiple new accounts just to show a credit history. If you have had little credit in the past, open no more than one or two accounts and build your history slowly.

DO NOT close old accounts. Length of credit history has a positive impact on your credit score. Having a large number of accounts in good standing with zero balances is a plus, not a negative.

Changing Your Debt Situation

DO reduce your balances on your credit cards and other loans. If you have a high outstanding balance on one or more of your credit cards, you will lose points on your score. Lower balances tend to lead to higher FICO® scores. Pay down your balances and keep them low.

DO NOT open new accounts to transfer high balances and spread your total debt across multiple accounts. If you feel you could benefit by moving a portion of the balance on one card to another, use an existing account. Of course, you would not want to move a balance from a low interest rate card to one that has a higher rate.

DO get help if you are having trouble paying your debts. It may be possible to have your debts renegotiated if you can show that your difficult financial situation is temporary and it can be improved over time. For example, you may have fallen behind in your bills because of unemployment but you are working again now. You can contact lenders directly or use a reputable not-for-profit credit-counseling agency. You are not asking your creditors for forgiveness here—you are just asking for a little more time. Your credit score is likely to be negatively affected if the lender agrees to write-off a portion of your debt. This is not true with a debt-management plan established with a credit-counseling agency. Working with a credit counseling program has a positive impact on your credit score over time as you regularly make your debt management plan payments.

DO pay off any late or written-off debt. These items will still stay on your credit report but the fact that you made good on the debt will be a plus.

DO re-establish your credit if you have had problems in the past. Opening one or two credit accounts and using them responsibly will slowly but surely rebuild your credit score. This may take a few years, however.

DO stop using your credit cards if you are not paying your balance in full each month. Using a card on which you carry a balance is almost guaranteed to result in ever-increasing balances.

DO NOT ignore debt problems. Credit scores can go down much faster than they can go up. Lenders typically report negative information right away. Again, contacting lenders directly or telephoning a reputable credit-counseling agency can be of help. Chapters 11 and 12 will provide additional information if you currently have serious debt problems.

DO NOT use repossession as a way to get out from under a debt. Repossession negatively affects credit scores even if the repossessed item has sufficient value to pay the debt. And in most cases its value is not enough to pay off the full balance owed. Thus you will still owe some amount of remaining debt. It would be better to sell the item yourself, add additional funds if necessary, and pay off the debt in full.

What You Can Do!

Action Module 10: Improving Your Credit Score

Now that you know some of the DO-s and DON'T-s of improving your credit score, its time to take action. The two worksheets below can help you chart a course towards a better credit score. The first will help you make sure you pay your bills on time. The second provides a checklist for the steps you want to take to build your credit score.

In addition to these worksheets, InCharge® Institute also offers educational tools and counseling services targeted specifically at improving your credit scores. You can receive a personalized credit analysis to help you understand your credit score and what it means. Most importantly you can obtain a customized plan to guide your use of credit in the future in order to boost your credit standing. **To learn more about this revolutionary service visit <u>www.brightscore.com</u>.**

Action Module 10A: The Bill Paying Calendar

Paying bills on time can go a long way toward increasing your credit score and keeping it high. But how can you manage that? One simple technique is to set up your bills as automatic payments from your checking account. Most utility companies and lenders have such plans. You may even receive a discount if you use this automatic system.

Another helpful method for paying bills on time is a bill-paying calendar as illustrated below. The purpose of such a calendar is to put your bill paying on a schedule that is easy to understand and follow. As indicated, you want to clearly see what bills you have on a regular basis, when they are due, when they should be sent, what is the typical amount and to check them off as they are paid.

You should keep the bill-paying calendar in a prominent place—perhaps taped to the side of your refrigerator.

Action Module 10A | The Bill Paying Calendar

My Bill-Paying Calendar for March				
Bill Name	Usual Due Date	Date to Be Mailed	Typical Amount	Date Actually Mailed
Example: Rent Payment	Last day of the month	March 24	$780	March 23

This worksheet is available for download at www.creditbooster.com/downloads/.

Action Module 10B: Credit Score Improvement Checklist

As you read through the first part of this chapter, you probably recognized a number of things you could DO to improve your credit score. Which ones were they? You also probably recognized some DO NOTs that you have been doing. Which ones were they? The checklist below can help you begin the process towards addressing these situations and improving your credit score.

Action Module 10B | Credit Score Improvement Checklist

My Credit Score Checklist		
Situation That Affects My Credit Score	Actions to Take?	Indicator That the Situation Has Changed
DO's That I will use in order to improve my credit score.		
Example: I am one month behind on my electric bill	*Stay up-to-date for one year.*	*I have stayed current on this account for 12 months.*
DO NOT's That I will avoid in order to improve my credit score (if I change the situation).		

This worksheet is available for download at www.creditbooster.com/downloads/.

Summary

- You can improve your FICO® score and thus enhance your eligibility for credit by fixing credit report mistakes

- Make all payments promptly. This will ensure that new, negative items do not appear on your account.

- Pay down existing credit balances.

- Do not add new accounts in order to lower balances on old accounts.

- Do not close long-term accounts

- Establish new credit, but only if you have little or no existing credit history.

- Use automatic payment plans or a bill paying calendar to ensure that all bills get paid on time.

- Taking actions to improve your credit score will be easier if you write down the specific item that is affecting your score, specify the action to take and identify how you will know that the situation has changed.

Section IV: The Fix is On! helps you begin the real work of taking the right steps necessary to improve your credit status. Chapter 10 focuses on improving your credit scores and provides you with information on how you can do even more to improve your credit status. *Chapter 11: Resolving Serious Credit Problems on Your Own!*, will provide you some guidance on things you can fix yourself.

BrightScore™

Put your credit improvement program into fast forward!

When it comes to getting the best interest rates on credit cards, car loans, mortgages and more, there's one number lenders use—your credit score. And if yours is lower than it should be because of errors in your *credit report, identity fraud,* or *accounts past due* or *in collections,* you're paying more than you should!

BrightScore™ is an interactive credit report and scoring program that gives you **customized, comprehensive guidance**—and **personalized recommendations** to boost your score—all while providing access to live phone-based counseling. You'll understand exactly what's in your credit report—and how it's impacting your score. With BrightScore™, you get:

- An easy-to-understand credit report and letter-grade score
- A personalized credit analysis and action plan, with customized recommendations
- A tool to help find and resolve errors
- Access to trained live BrightScore™ counselors

Learn more about a BrightScore™ solution today—online at www.creditbooster.com or call toll-free: 1-888-801-0384.

In **CreditBooster**™ *Section IV* you are focusing on actions you can take to improve your financial status. In Chapter 7 you established specific goals. In Chapter 8, you developed a budget. In Chapter 9 you learned how to remove mistakes from your credit report. Then in Chapter 10 you learned ways to improve your credit score. All of these steps will improve your credit status.

But what if your debts are more than you can handle now? What if you just do not have enough income to pay the monthly bills? What if you have never paid a bill late but you are worried that is going to happen soon? What can be done to get your debts under control and restore your good credit?

There are two approaches available to you. The first involves steps you can take on your own to make your debts more manageable. This do-it-yourself approach is the focus of Chapter 11.

What You Need To Know!

Being overly indebted and financially distressed can be one of the most difficult problems ever faced by individuals and families. Excess debt not only affects one's day-to-day financial life, but it often causes emotional stress for everyone in a household. Some people do not realize the full impact of their negative emotions about debt problems. Being seriously in debt causes stress. It often hurts marriages and other family relationships. Many people bring their financial stresses to the workplace. Others sometimes manage high debt levels for years until illness, loss of overtime, or job loss pushes them over the edge.

Preventing excess debt through sound financial management practices is the best approach to getting through life successfully. As you have gone through the various modules in **CreditBooster**™, you have learned many of these practices. But what if you are in financial trouble now and want to do something about it yourself? There are steps that you can take to get back to financial health.

Eight Steps to Taking Control of Your Personal Finances

There are eight options that people with too much debt can take to bring their financial lives back under control. Taking these actions quickly, at the first sign of financial difficulty, is a key to eventual success. Regardless of where you are in your financial life, these eight steps will help you take control of your personal finances and keep you on the path of being financially successful...forever.

Step One:

ADMIT THE FINANCIAL PROBLEMS TO YOURSELF AND YOUR LOVED ONES – Denial only makes debt problems worse. Perhaps you recognized that you have some debt problems when you calculated your financial ratios in Chapter 4. Perhaps your debt payments-to-take-home pay ratio was over 20 percent. Perhaps your debt service-to-gross income ratio was over 36 percent. Now is the time to revisit Chapter 4 to see if you may be carrying too much debt. If you and your loved ones recognize that you have too much debt, you can begin to take actions to change your situation. It oftentimes takes efforts of every family member to get out of debt and on the road to financial success.

Step Two:

QUIT BORROWING MONEY – It seems obvious that you cannot borrow your way out of debt. However, many people try. They seem to think that the next loan will put them in a better situation. Borrowing more money than necessary to pay off a debt means you are going backward, not forward, financially.

Credit cards are a big problem for people in this regard. It is so easy to use credit cards to smooth out the tight financial times. Things might appear to be okay if you are paying your minimum credit card payments on time. Certainly, the credit card company is happy if you are.

They should be. When you are paying the minimum payment on a card that you continue to use, you are borrowing more per month than you are actually paying on the account. As a result, your debt is rising and so is the interest they will receive. Consider this illustration:

As of 2005, most credit cards have a minimum monthly payment of 4 percent of the amount owed. If you owe $1000 on a credit card, the minimum payment is $40 ($1000 x 0.04).

If the card has an APR of 18 percent, the interest for the month is $15 ($1000 x 0.18/12). When you make the minimum payment of $40 you will be paying only $25 toward the principal amount of $1000.

$25 is very little to pay toward principle. At that rate it will take you 7 years and 3 months to pay off the $1000 debt and you will pay an extra $515.60 in interest for a total repayment amount of $1,515.60. In fact, it may take you much longer! Paying it off in 7 years and 3 months will only happen if you stop using the card. If you use the card by charging more things this month, you will need to pay the full amount of the new purchase plus the $40 minimum payment due in order to pay the original principle of $1000 off in 7 years and 3 months.

No one wants to stay in debt to a credit card company for more than 7 years. The only solution is to quit borrowing money by charging new purchases on the card and pay more than the minimum required payment each month.

Step Three:

SPEND LESS AND EARN MORE – Too much debt means that your spending has exceeded your income for some time, perhaps a long time. Maybe it is time to do the opposite. Perhaps it is time to cut spending to the bare minimum. Examine every variable expense category in your budget to see if you can reduce spending. You can allocate even $10 from each toward debt payment. Then look at your fixed expenses, too. Could you drop one or more of your telephone services—either a cell phone or the local phone service into your home? Then allocate the reductions to debt payment. Increasing your income can help too. Could you take a second job? Could you work overtime? Working more can help get your debts under control.

The extra hours need not be a permanent situation. You might decide to work extra and earn more income for six months to help pay off your debts. Perhaps you could set aside ten percent of the extra income to reward yourself with a weekend vacation when your debts are under control.

Step Four:

FOCUS YOUR SPENDING PLAN ON JUST ONE GOAL—DEBT REPAYMENT – In Chapter 6, you established some financial goals. Then in Chapter 8, you developed a Spending Plan to reach those goals. The principle behind that Plan was the concept of "paying yourself first." Yet having excess debt is the opposite of paying yourself first. You are paying your creditors first and doing so in two ways. One, you are paying on the debt itself. Two, you are paying interest.

Would you be willing to borrow on a credit card at 15 percent in order to invest in the stock market at 10 percent? Of course you would not. You would clearly see that you are losing money on such an arrangement. Yet that is exactly what people who are saving for various goals do while carrying excessive credit card and other debt.

All of the goals you listed in Chapter 6 are good ones. But if your debt levels are too high, you need to focus on just one goal—debt repayment.

Step Five:

RESTRUCTURE YOUR DEBT – All debts are not the same. The difference is the interest rate being charged. **You should repay the debts with the highest interest rates first.** Why? Because they cost you the most money. You may need to make just the minimum payments on the other debts in order to focus on paying off the high–interest rate debts. This is a good strategy. You save interest this way. Of course, this will only work if you stop running up the balance on the credit card.

Here is an example of how debt restructuring might work:

Martina Johnson prepared Table 11.1 as her debt inventory (recall your own debt inventory from Chapter 1). Martina set a goal of paying off all her credit cards within three years.

- Martina has a personal loan that has to be paid off in seven years, with an initial balance of $5000 and which has been paid down to $4690.

- She owes a total of $9500 on her five credit cards ($1,100 + $1,500 + $500 + $4,800 + $1,600).

- Assuming that Martina does not use the cards again, the total monthly payments on all her debts are $421.93.

- The interest portion of the payments for the next month will total about $174.

- Only $248 of the payments will actually go to pay off the debts.

Action Module 11.1 | Debt Inventory for Martina Johnson - Before Adjustments/Transfers

Account	Limit	APR	Balance	Payoff Date (in months)	Monthly Payment	Interest Portion of Payment*	Principal Portion of Payment**	Comments
Personal Loan	$5,000	9%	$4,690	77	$80.44	$35 17	$45.27	Low APR
Credit Card #1 (joint account)	$5,000	12%	$1,100	36	$36 53	$11.00	$25 53	Low APR, available balance
Credit Card #2	$1,500	10%	$1,500	36	$48.40	$12 50	$35.90	Annual Fee $50
Credit Card #3	$3,000	14%	$500	36	$17.09	$5 83	$11.26	Low APR available balance
Credit Card #4	$6 000	20%	$4,800	36	$178.37	$80.00	$98.37	High APR, high balance
Credit Card #5	$3,000	22%	$1,600	36	$61.10	$29.33	$31.77	High APR, low balance
TOTAL	$23,500		$14,190		$421.93	$173.83	$248.10	High Paymets, high interest

*Interest portion of each payment is calculated by multiplying the APR (as a decimal–9% = 09) times the balance divided by 12

**Principal portion of each payment is calculated by subtracteing the interest portion from the monthly payment.

Martina sat down at her kitchen table to try and figure out what she could do to lower her monthly payments and have a higher percentage of the repayments go toward paying off the debt instead of going mostly toward interest. She also wanted to lower the average APR. Here is her plan:

1. Martina realized that she could transfer debt from the highest-APR cards to the lowest-APR cards. To do so, however, she needed a higher debt limit on her joint account card. So, she requested an increase from $5000 to $7000.

2. She then used balance transfers to pay off fully cards 2, 4, and 5. She transferred the balances to cards 1 and 3. Even though card 2 had the lowest APR, the fact that it was maxed out and had a high annual fee made it a poor choice for a balance transfer.

3. Martina kept card 5 open for convenience uses (which will be discussed later). The card has a grace period for new purchases, so there will be no interest charges as long as she pays the balance is paid in full each month.

4. Martina then revised her debt inventory. She decided that it would be difficult to pay off the new balance on the joint account card in 36 months, so she extended the projected payoff for that card to 48 months.

Action Module 11.2 illustrates Martina's revised debt inventory.

- She was able to reduce the monthly payments to $353.34, a savings of more than $68 per month ($421.93 - $353.34 = $68.59).

- She was able to reduce the interest portion of these payments to approximately $135.

- The payment toward the principal of the debts went down to $218.34, about $30 less than before. If Martina chose, she could apply that extra $30 to card 1 and pay it off in just under 3 years.

Martina's plan simply rearranged the debts to get the balances owed on the lowest-APR opportunities available. Martina also could have asked for an increase in the limit on the home-equity loan. If home-equity debt payments become too difficult to repay, she could lose her home to foreclosure.

Action Module 11.2 | Revised Debt Inventory for Marina Johnson - After Adjustment/Transfers

Account	Limit	APR	Balance	Payoff Date (in months)	Monthly Payment	Interest Portion of Payment*	Principal Portion of Payment**	Comments
Personal Loan	$5,000	9%	$4,690	77	$80.44	$35.17	$45.27	Low APR
Credit Card #1 (joint account)	$7,000	12%	$6,600	48	$173.78	$66.00	$107.78	Low APR, small available balance
Credit Card #2	$0	10%	$0		$0	$0	$0	
Credit Card #3	$3 000	14%	$2,900	36	$99.12	$33.83	$65.29	Low APR, no available balance
Credit Card #4	$0	20%	$0		$0			
Credit Card #5	$3,000	22%	$0		$0			Account paid off Use but carry no balance
TOTAL	$18,000		$14,190		$353.34	$135.00	$218.34	Lower payments, lower interest

*Interest portion of each payment is calculated by multiplying the APR (as a decimal–9% = .09) times the
  balance divided by 12
**Principal portion of each payment is calculated by subtracteing the interest portion from the monthly payment.

Note that Martina decided not to close two of her accounts. As you learned in Chapter 10, closing accounts can lead to a reduction in one's credit score. She must resist the temptation to use those cards if her finances get tight.

When people have too much debt, the goal of getting and staying out of debt outweighs the goal of maintaining one's credit score. This is because the credit score will be more severely impacted by failure to pay debts.

Step Six:

REFINANCE ONE OR MORE DEBTS – Debt refinancing entails taking out a new loan to replace another. The goal is usually to take advantage of lower interest rates that might be available as compared to those available when the first loan was granted. Refinancing of home mortgages is common.

Is refinancing an option for you? Perhaps, but here are some notes of caution:

- Refinance a loan primarily to obtain the lower monthly payments that result from the lower interest rate. Avoid refinancing for a higher loan balance than is owed on the original loan. Doing so is called an "add-on" loan. For example, you might owe $100,000 on your home mortgage but could qualify to refinance for $120,000. The extra $20,000 is very tempting, but it adds to your overall debt burden.

- If you do refinance for more than the amount owed on the original loan, use the additional funds ($20,000 in the example above) to pay off other debts. And only do so if the new loan has a lower interest rate than the loans to be paid off. This same caution applies if you are taking out a second mortgage on your home to pay off other debts. These additional funds should not be spent.

- Avoid refinancing for a longer time period than remains on the original loan. This too will lower your monthly payment but will result in more total interest being repaid over the life of the loan. This same caution applies if you are taking out a second mortgage on your home to pay off other debts.

- Recognize that when you refinance a home mortgage to obtain additional funds to pay off credit cards, you are replacing short-term debt for long-term debt. Pay extra on the new loan for a time to bring the balance down to only what was owed on the home. Also recognize that you are replacing debt that has no collateral with debt that has your home as collateral. If you fail to pay, you can lose your house.

- Be wary of the various costs and fees associated with refinancing. Lenders can offer lower interest rates if they collect some funds up front. Compare APRs and not the quoted interest rate.

Debt consolidation loans are not the same as refinancing. These loans are often offered to people in credit trouble as a way to pay off all debts in return "for one low monthly payment." In most cases such loans have a lower payment only because the time period of the loan is longer. Debt consolidation loans often have higher interest rates, not lower.

Step Seven:

COMMUNICATE WITH YOUR CREDITORS – Many people think that their lenders will fail to notice financial difficulties that are building if customers avoid calling attention to them. But in the computerized world of credit today, lenders are keenly aware of your debt situation. Lenders are fully aware of their customers' payment and borrowing patterns on accounts with that creditor. They also know the patterns with other lenders as well.

This is especially true for credit card lenders. Credit card companies routinely request credit reports on their current customers to ensure that the customer is not getting in credit difficulty that would put repayment at risk on the company's account. So there is no point in hiding from your creditors.

If your problems are not too severe and you are still current on your accounts, you should ask for a lower interest rate on your accounts as Martina Johnson did in Step 4 above. Getting a lower interest rate will reduce your monthly payment, and you can either keep paying the old amount to pay off the debt more quickly or you could apply the savings to another credit account that you want to repay.

If your credit problems are serious and you are late with your repayments or skipping them altogether, you will not be able to get a lower interest rate on a card. But you should let the lender know why you are having such difficulty. Perhaps the lender might agree to stretch the payments out for a longer time period. You might be able to persuade the lender to accept payment of interest only for a few months. It never hurts to ask a creditor for some special assistance.

If you are in serious financial trouble, you might be able to persuade the lender to accept less than the total amount owed. In other words, the lender might be willing to forgive part of the debt. You might owe $2,000 and the lender might accept only $1,700 if you can pay that amount in full. Getting something is better, for the lender, than getting nothing in such cases.

These latter situations where payments are being missed or have stopped altogether are not ones you can usually deal with on your own. In such cases, you will need the assistance of a professional credit counselor. How to use a credit counselor to help you deal with debt problems is the subject of Chapter 12.

Step Eight:

SELL SOME ASSETS – Many people who are in debt have significant assets, too. Look at your balance sheet from Chapter 2. Are there assets you could cash in or sell to raise funds? You should first look at your use assets. Perhaps you have an extra vehicle or some recreational equipment such as a boat that could be sold to pay down your debt. Do you have funds in a savings account that might be used? There is no point in paying 18 percent interest on a credit card debt while you have money in a savings account earning only 2 percent. One asset you would not want to touch is a retirement account at your place of employment, however. Retirement savings is to be used only for your future financial security, so you should never borrow those funds to repay consumer debts. (Retirement funds also are excluded in a bankruptcy proceeding.)

What You Can Do!

Action Module 11A: My Revised Debt Inventory

As you can see from the list above, there are many options you can take to resolve credit problems on your own. The first four items all involve adjusting your budget in some way to reflect the debt difficulties you face. You will want to refer back to Chapter 8 and revise your budget as necessary.

Steps 5-8 above will require some thinking on your part. Not all steps may be necessary, and some aspects of each may not be appropriate for your situation. *Action Modules 11A-D* can help you decide what steps will work for you.

Restructuring Your Debt

In Chapter 1 you developed a debt inventory. You listed all your debts and for each debt recorded the interest rate, balance owed, payoff date, and monthly payment. As described in Step 5 above—Restructure Your Debt—you might benefit from restructuring one or more debts so that your overall debt payment amounts and interest paid each month are reduced. Step 5 provides an example of how this might be accomplished. Now it is your turn. You can use *Action Module 11A: My Revised Debt Inventory* to revise your debt inventory. You might need to refer back to Chapter 1 to do some of the calculations.

Action Module 11A | My Revised Debt Inventory

Debts	#1	#2	#3	#4	#5	#6
Account						
Limit						
APR						
Balance						
Payoff Date (in months)						
New Monthly Payment*						
Interest Portion of Payment*						
Principal Portion of Payment**						
Comments						

*Interest portion of each payment is calculated by multiplying the APR (as a decimal–9%= 09) times the balance divided by 12
**Principal portion of each payment is calculated by subtracting the interest portion from the monthly payment.

This worksheet is available for download at www.creditbooster.com/downloads/

Action Module 11B: Refinancing Your Debt

Step 6 above—Refinancing Debt—discusses the benefits of refinancing one or more of your debts. The goals of Step 6 are to reduce monthly payments and lower overall interest charges. The decision to refinance a debt can be complicated. Most lenders will outline the process for you and let you know how much you might save by refinancing before you have to commit to the new loan. There are also calculators on the Internet at sites such as bankrate.com and money.com that you can use to make the decision. ***Action Module 11B: My Refinancing Worksheet*** can help you organize your thoughts in preparation for this more detailed analysis.

Action Module 11B | My Refinancing Worksheet

	Factor	Factor	Factor	Factor	Factor	Factor
Debt/Balance	*Example: Home Mortgage/ $127 000*					
Old APR/ New APR	*7.5%/6 25%*					
Old Term/ New Term	*23 years/ 20 years*					
Additional Funds That Could be Generated to Pay Other Debts	*$13,000*					
Old Payment/ New Payment	*$1023/$957*					
Other Debt to Be Paid/Balance	*Credit Card #2/$14 000*					
APR on Other Debt	*16%*					
Term of Other Debt	*Indefinite*					

This worksheet is available for download at www.creditbooster.com/downloads/.

The primary benefit from refinancing debt is the lower monthly payments and lower monthly interest charges that result from the lower interest rate on the new loan. However, if you refinance for a longer time period (which also helps lower the monthly payment) you may pay higher TOTAL interest charges over the longer time period of the new loan.

Action Module 11C: Communicating With Your Lenders

Step 7—Communicate With Your Lenders—discusses how you can communicate with lenders when your debts become unmanageable. Perhaps you could request a lower interest rate or an extension on the loan.

Action Module 11C provides a table that you can use to keep track of your contacts with lenders. It will help you two ways. First, it lets you plan your requests and contacts. Second, it provides a record of your efforts should you need to later verify the results of your requests.

Action Module 11C | My Creditor Contact and Results

Debt	Problem in Need of Resolution	Request to Make of The Lender	Contact Name	Date of Last Contact	Response Received
Example: Credit Card #4	*High Monthly Interest*	*Request Lower Interest Rate*	*Ms. J. Martin*	*May 23, 2004*	*Rate will be lowered from $15% to 12%*

This worksheet is available for download at www.creditbooster.com/downloads/

Action Module 11D: Selling Assets

Step 8—Selling Assets—-discusses the benefits of cashing in or selling one or more assets in order to reduce your debt load. Look back to the balance sheet you prepared in Chapter 2. Are there assets you could sell? *Action Module 11D* provides a worksheet you could use to decide whether to cash in or sell any assets in order to reduce your debts.

Action Module 11D | Assets You Might Sell To Pay Off Debt

Asset	Current Dollar Value	Available Dollar Value After Paying Any Debt on the Asset	Debt to Which the Funds Will be Applied (in decending APR order)	Amount Owed On the Debt	APR on the Debt
Example: Motorcycle	*$5,500*	*$3,700*	*Credit Card #1*	*$4,000*	*17%*

This worksheet is available for download at www.creditbooster.com/downloads/.

The primary benefit of selling assets to pay off debt is the resulting lower balances on those debts and thus the lower monthly payments and reduced interest charges.

Summary

- Problems with excessive debt should not be ignored. The sooner you address the problem the better.

- If you find yourself with excessive debt you should direct all budget activity towards paying down your debts.

- Some debts can be restructured by moving balances to lower rate accounts and closing accounts as necessary.

- It may be possible to refinance some debts to obtain a lower interest rate and reduce monthly payments. In some cases you may want to borrow an additional amount when refinancing and use the funds to pay off a higher cost debt.

- When debt repayment becomes difficult and payments are being made late or not at all, you should communicate your difficulties to your creditors to see if alternative payment plans can be worked out.

- If possible, you can sell assets to pay off debts quickly.

Section IV: The Fix is On! helps you begin the real work of taking the right steps necessary to improve your credit status. Chapter 10 focuses on improving your credit scores and provides you with information on how you can do even more to improve your credit status. Chapter 11 provides you some guidance on things you can fix yourself. *Chapter 12: Getting Help for Resolving Serious Debt Problems* provides some direction where to go when you can't fix things yourself.

What if your debts are more than you can handle now? What if you just do not have enough income to pay the monthly bills? What if you have never paid a bill late but you are worried that is going to happen soon? What can be done to get your debts under control and restore your good credit?

Chapter 11 discussed do-it-yourself steps you can take on your own to make your debts more manageable. This chapter will provide guidance, when you encounter financial problems you cannot fix yourself, on how you can obtain outside assistance with debt problems.

What You Need To Know!

People with serious debt problems often find that they are unable or not confident enough to solve their problems on their own. Instead, they would like to find a reputable, qualified individual or organization that could provide such assistance. Fortunately, such outside assistance is available today. Unfortunately, many who provide such assistance are unqualified, unethical, or simply do not provide the right kind of assistance to meet particular needs of these people.

There are basically four different sources of outside help for anyone with serious debt problems:

1. **DEBT CONSOLIDATION LENDERS** – These organizations focus on marketing debt consolidation loans as a way to resolve debt difficulties. In theory, debt consolidation does have its benefits. This is a good option if you are able to consolidate the debts at a much lower interest rate. You trade many monthly payments for one payment that is lower than all the others combined. However, a high percentage of people who choose this option find themselves even deeper in debt one or two years later. The major reason is that they continue to borrow money to cover expenses. Remember, debt consolidation does not PAY OFF debt. It simply puts all or most debt into one basket. And a debt consolidation loan is often a very high cost way to borrow money.

2. **DEBT SETTLEMENT COMPANIES** – Debt settlement companies negotiate with lenders to accept only a portion of the amount owed and forgive the remaining debt. They often charge a considerable fee and claim to be able to obtain an immediate reduction in monthly payments. The reality of debt settlement is that the consumer is told to stop paying his bills and payments for about three or four months so the client can build a sizeable "pot" of money. The debt settlement company then tries to negotiate a payoff amount with each creditor, using the threat of the person going bankrupt as a negotiating tool.

Say the person owes $10,000. Instead of making payments for three months, he or she saves the money—perhaps accumulating $3000. The debt settlement company takes a $500 fee and pushes creditors to accept the remaining $2500. This results in only 25 cents being paid for each dollar owed. This might appear to be an attractive way out of debt difficulty, but such an arrangement basically destroys the client's credit history and credit score. The unpaid debts stay on his or her credit report for seven years.

3. **BANKRUPTCY COURT** – Under bankruptcy, all or a portion of one's debts can be absolved by the courts. Bankruptcy should be a last resort. There are considerable complications to the process and the attorney fees can be expensive. Further, bankruptcy stays on one's credit history for ten years.

4. **CREDIT COUNSELING SERVICES** – There are two principal ways that credit-counseling organizations provide assistance to debtors. The first involves working closely with consumers to help them get their financial lives under control. This might include such services as budgeting assistance, financial education and counseling for the emotional side of debt problems.

The second major way that credit counseling organizations provide assistance is through a debt management program (DMP). In a DMP, the credit counseling organization works with lenders to rearrange and adjust the client's debt to make it more manageable for clients. DMPs will not affect your credit score (see Chapter 10). However, your lenders may place a notation in your credit bureau file; and it may affect some lenders' decisions about granting you credit.

What Are Credit Counseling Services?

If you have trouble controlling your debts or cannot negotiate with creditors, it is a relief to know that you can always find assistance from a credit counseling organization. Reputable and professional not-for-profit credit counseling organizations exist to help people just like you regain control of their debts and their lives.

There are two types of organizations that provide credit counseling services:

- **FOR-PROFIT BUSINESSES ASSIST PEOPLE WHOSE DEBTS HAVE BECOME PROBLEMATIC** – A number of for-profit organizations have been criticized for not delivering good value for the money spent by the clients. And in some states, "for-profit credit counseling" is illegal.

- **NOT-FOR-PROFIT CREDIT COUNSELING ORGANIZATIONS PROVIDE COUNSELING AND DEBT MANAGEMENT SERVICES, AND THEY TYPICALLY CHARGE LOW FEES** – Sometimes they waive all fees. Credit counseling assists people just like you in dealing with financial stress, making a workable budget, bringing credit accounts up to date, resolving specific credit problems, and making a plan to get out of debt. Non-profit credit counseling organizations offer counseling and education on budgeting, debt, and personal finance.

  Some credit counseling companies require that you meet with them face-to-face, which requires you telephone them for an appointment and then travel to their location for a one-on-one counseling session. You may not get an appointment for a week or two.

  Other credit counseling companies provide immediate assistance for consumers by telephone. Here there is no need to make an appointment a few weeks in the future or to arrange for transportation to the company's office. Millions of overly indebted consumers have found that telephoning a not-for-profit credit counseling company for help is a major convenience. For an example of the services provided by not-for-profit credit counseling organization, you may contact InCharge® Debt Solutions by telephoning, toll-free 1-866-254-8925 or visit their web site at www.incharge.org.

  Most not-for-profit credit counseling organizations offer a Debt Management Program (DMP) as a way to help you get out of debt faster and with a lot less hassle. They have a strong commitment to personal finance education for their clients so that debt problems stay away once they are solved. And they also have a strong commitment to provide personal finance education to the American public at large, so they can attain/maintain their financial "wellness," whether they need a DMP or not.

What is a Debt Management Program?

Under a Debt Management Program (DMP), the non-profit credit counseling organization will negotiate with your creditors for lower interest rates and lower payments on unsecured debts. Most DMPs only address debt that is not backed by collateral. Auto and mortgage loans, for example, generally cannot be re-aged through a DMP. Nonetheless, a DMP can be helpful in getting your credit card and other unsecured debt under control.

Credit counseling companies will also negotiate with creditors to re-age your debts. That is, the creditor waives administrative fees and late charges and brings your credit account up to date. You make a monthly payment to the credit counseling service, which then disburses payments to all of your creditors who have agreed to the plan. A DMP helps consumers pay off all their debts in as few as three or four years, rather than ten or more years that it takes for people not enrolled in a DMP program.

A DMP is not a debt consolidation loan. It is a way out of debt.

Not-for-profit credit counseling organizations offer a significant advantage over doing it yourself. The other educational and counseling services provided by the non-profit credit counseling organization most likely outweigh this factor, but you should consider it when deciding to use a non-profit credit counseling organization.

If you do your own negotiating, it is possible that you might be able to negotiate repayment of some of your debts for less than you owe. You should understand that this would likely be included in your credit report as an unpaid debt. The effect would be the same as if you had used the services of a debt settlement company.

How Credit Counseling Companies Serve the Public and Make Money

Credit counseling companies typically charge a small voluntary setup contribution of $75 or less and a voluntary monthly maintenance contribution of $50 or less. These not-for-profit companies are also supported by voluntary contributions from creditors. Credit counseling organizations often receive a small percentage of the funds paid by clients to the creditors. Creditors agree to do this because they realize they are more likely to get paid when their clients are working with a credit counselor.

It is important to note that the consumer does not pay this contribution. Most creditors are willing to pay the contribution to the credit counseling service because they want clients to repay their debts instead of declaring bankruptcy. When a consumer files for bankruptcy, unsecured creditors such as credit card companies usually get very little if any of their money back.

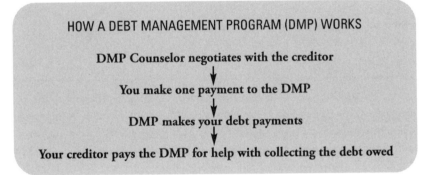

HOW A DEBT MANAGEMENT PROGRAM (DMP) WORKS

DMP Counselor negotiates with the creditor
↓
You make one payment to the DMP
↓
DMP makes your debt payments
↓
Your creditor pays the DMP for help with collecting the debt owed

How Debt Management Programs (DMP) Work

In the illustration below, the arrows represent payments to the same four creditors. With a Debt Management Program (DMP), the borrower makes only one monthly payment to the credit counseling company that is then distributed to those same four creditors.

A Before and After Example of a Debt Management Program

BEFORE DMP		AFTER DMP
$8,000	**Principal Owed**	$8,000
$254/month	**Payment**	$254/month
$4,700 - $9,000	**Total Interest Paid**	$1,398
5-15 years	**Out of Debt In**	3 years

Note that total interest paid and years to get out of debt are far lower when using the Debt Management Program. The reasons are twofold. First, counselors negotiate lower interest rates on your behalf so more of every dollar goes toward repaying principal instead of interest. The result is a faster payoff on the debt, as indicated by the arrow above. Next, in the Debt Management Program you pay a constant $254 per month (as circled) throughout the program. Without a Debt Management Program, as the debt is paid down, the minimum required monthly payment goes down as well. Most consumers would then reduce their monthly payments. When you only pay the minimum on this much credit card debt, it could take 15 years or more to pay off the balance. This could result in interest payments of perhaps $9,000 over all those years.

What Should You Look for When Choosing a Credit Counseling Service

If you decide that using a credit counseling service would be beneficial to you, you will need to choose one that is reputable and meets your specific needs. You can find a professional credit counseling service on the Internet by searching for the phrase "credit counseling services." You can also find credit counseling services in the Yellow Pages of your telephone book by looking under the heading "Credit and Debt Counseling Services." Note that the listings will include profit and not-for-profit agencies. And you would have no way of telling which are reputable. But at least you will have a list of agencies to contact.

You could also contact the Association of Independent Consumer Credit Counseling Agencies (AICCCA) or the National Foundation for Consumer Credit (NFCC) for suggestions of credit counseling services that might meet your needs.

Consider these areas when evaluating a particular credit counseling service:

REPUTATION

The best credit counseling services take pride in their reputation. They belong to one of the two prominent trade groups in the field—the Association of Independent Consumer Credit Counseling Agencies (AICCCA) or the National Foundation for Consumer Credit (NFCC). They also belong to the Better Business Bureau. You might also contact your state's consumer protection agency (look under "consumer protection" in the government pages of your phone book) for a business reputation report. These items are not a guarantee of the credit counseling organization's reputation. But having good standing on all of these items is a good sign.

QUALIFICATIONS

The counselors employed by the credit counseling service should be highly qualified and well-trained. A qualified organization can accomplish this by having an outside group certify its counselors. For example, the Association for Financial Counseling and Planning Education grants the Accredited Credit Counselor (ACC) designation to counselors who have passed a certification exam, have six months of documented experience, agree to earn 15 Continuing Education Units every two years, and agree to a code of ethics.

COST

Reputable credit counseling services do not charge excessive fees. This is because they are effective at helping people manage their debts and creditors are willing to pay fair share reimbursements to the service. Always ask the credit counseling service about their typical initial and monthly contributions. Also ask if the contributions are voluntary—they should not be charging mandatory fees. Be wary if the credit counselor quickly pushes you to pay a set-up contribution in excess of $75 and monthly contributions of more than $50.

SERVICES PROVIDED

Reputable credit counseling services have a wide range of services. They do not rely solely on debt management plans when assisting their clients. The counselor should spend enough time with you to understand your situation—perhaps an hour or more on the initial call. He or she should fully explore your debts and your income and tell you how much lower your monthly payments will be and how long it will take to pay off your debts. Finally, he or she should conduct business with you in a way that is convenient for you not him or her. For example, would you prefer face-to-face meetings, telephone conferences, or working through the Internet?

Finally, you should never agree to a debt management plan until you know the exact amount of your new payment and how long you will need to stay in the plan to get your debts paid off. Keep paying your bills yourself until you know that the service has begun making payments. You can call your creditors to determine if payments are being made on your behalf through the debt management plan.

What You Can Do!

Action Module 12: Getting Help for Debt Problems

Now that you understand the services offered by a credit counseling service, you need to decide if this option is right for you. The decision will be based on how serious your debt problems are and whether you feel confident about taking the do-it-yourself approach outlined in Chapter 11.

Do you have what it takes to negotiate with creditors, start a budget that really works, and then exercise control every aspect of your spending? Be honest! If so, go for it.

If your candid evaluation is that you cannot do this on your own, don't be discouraged. Get thee to a credit counselor!

You will want to contact several credit counseling services to find one that is right for you.

You can use the checklist below to compare the services you are considering. Unless otherwise noted, the best answer for each question is "yes."

Action Module 12A | My Credit Counseling Service Checklist

Criteria	Service #1	Service #2	Service #3	Service #4
Does the service operate on a not-for-profit basis?				
Are the counselors certified by a third party organization?				
Is a full range of solutions-based services discussed rather than focusing exclusively on a debt management program?				
Did the counselor take the time to answer your questions and thoroughly explore your situation?				
Do counselors receive bonuses or commissions for signing people up for a debt management program rather than simply education and counseling services? The best answer is "No."				
Does the service receive a portion of its budget from contribution funds paid by lenders?				
Does the service work with the creditors who do not pay the contribution as well as those who do?				
What is the initial setup contribution for a client entering the debt management plan?				
What is the monthly contribution for a client in a debt management program?				
Are the contributions voluntary?				
How soon will I get out of debt?				
Does the organization also push debt consolidation loans? The best answer is "No"				

This worksheet is available for download at www.creditbooster.com/downloads/

Summary

- Credit counseling services provide budgeting, financial education and debt counseling services as well as more formal debt management plans.

- A debt management program results in lower interest rates and thus lower payments on your debts as well as reduced late and other penalties on problems debts. Debt management plans are not loans and do not reduce the amounts owed.

- Non-profit credit counseling services are paid via initial, low-cost set-up and monthly fees paid by clients and through "fair share" amounts paid by creditors.

- The counselors employed by a credit counseling service should be certified by an independent third-party organization.

Now we are ready to focus on some special credit cases—building credit when you don't have any (in Chapter 13), how divorce affects your credit (in Chapter 14), and how you can rebuild credit after bankruptcy (Chapter 15).

Chapter 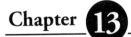 13 | Building Credit When You Do Not Have Any

Section IV: The Fix Is On! helped you begin the real work of taking the right steps necessary to improve your credit status. Chapter 10 focused on improving your credit scores and provided you with information on how you can do even more to improve your credit status. Chapter 11 provided you some guidance on things you can fix yourself. Chapter 12 provided some direction where to go when you can't fix things yourself.

Now we are ready to focus on some special credit cases—building credit when you don't have any (in Chapter 13), how divorce affects your credit (in Chapter 14), and how you can rebuild credit after bankruptcy (Chapter 15).

What You Need To Know!

Remember when you were looking for your first job? Employers wanted to know about your previous work experiences. You probably wondered how you could have experience if you had never had a job. You probably thought employers were being unfair.

Building a credit history is somewhat like those first job searches. You can't build a credit history until someone gives you credit. Yet, in order to get credit, you must first have good credit experiences. You might think that is unfair, too. Fortunately, there are several things you can do to build good credit, even if you have never had credit at all.

Is No Credit the Same as Bad Credit?

To answer this question, think back to the 5 C's of Credit discussed in Chapter 1:

- Capacity
- Capital
- Conditions
- Collateral
- Character

It is the fifth of the 5 C's, Character, that is a problem for people who are new to the world of credit. This is not to say that they have bad character. They may be very trustworthy. What it means is that they cannot use prior success in handling credit as evidence that they are trustworthy. It is their "credit" character that is in question, not their personal character.

So, is no credit worse than bad credit? If you have no credit history at all, creditors may treat you the same as if you have bad credit. They will ask the same question they ask of all borrowers—will I get my money back? Their uncertainty may seem unfair. But, in reality, you have not established a history to show that you have the discipline to make payments over an extended period of time. Lenders simply have no way of knowing that you are trustworthy.

Fortunately, you can fix having a no-credit history faster that you can repair a bad credit record. To establish good credit, you can focus on the other four C's of credit: capacity, capital, conditions, and collateral. These four areas are the keys to getting credit when you have never had credit before:

- Can you show that you have the income needed to make debt payments—Capacity?
- Do you have sufficient financial worth to be able to carry a debt—Capital?
- Do lenders have funds available to lend to you—Conditions?
- Are you able to pledge an asset to help secure the debt—Collateral?

As you can see below there is more you can do in each of these four areas.

Building Your Capacity

Capacity refers to having sufficient income to afford the payments that would be required on a loan or credit card account. Lenders look for people who have a steady job and who have shown that they can keep a job. Part-time work and frequent job changes will work against you.

People with higher incomes are seen as having higher capacity to make credit payments. Can you ask for a raise or a promotion at work? Could you add hours to your schedule? An added benefit of having additional income is that you may not need to borrow as much when you do take out a loan.

Another way that lenders judge capacity is how well you pay your monthly bills. If you can't make ends meet and are late or skip payments for phone, cable and utility bills the lender will wonder whether you have the income necessary to pay on a credit contract. Many people do not realize that having a cell phone builds good credit. That is because cell phone companies report bill paying patterns to the major credit bureaus. Make sure you pay all bills on time and in full.

Finally, you want to be able to show that you can handle the money you do have. One way that lenders can judge this is whether or not you frequently write bad checks or otherwise overdraw your checking account. You can ask your bank about overdraft protection to make sure that you do not.

Building Your Capital

Capital refers to your overall level of wealth. Lenders want to know that you would still have sufficient financial assets to make credit payments should your income go down. One way to show this is to have money in the bank. If you do not already have them, you should open both a checking account and a savings account. Then have your paycheck deposited into your accounts directly, allocating a portion of your check into checking to cover your monthly expenses and putting the remainder in your savings account. Over time, try to build a sufficient savings account balance to cover two or three month's worth of expenses. This "emergency fund" will look good to lenders.

You might also want to purchase a certificate of deposit (CD) at your bank. A CD is a type of savings account where you agree to leave the money untouched for a fixed period of time such as six months or one or more years. Lenders sometimes look on CDs positively because they know you will not be spending the money anytime soon.

Take Advantage of Conditions

Conditions refers to the availability of money to lend, usually because of the condition of the national economy. During times of economic prosperity, lenders are more willing to loan money both because money is more available and because there is less likelihood that borrowers will lose their jobs. While you cannot do anything about the national economy, you can recognize when credit might be easier to obtain.

Related to the national economy are the conditions being faced by certain types of lenders. Retail stores frequently are more willing to loan money or offer credit cards when they are trying to increase sales. Automobile dealers and manufacturers may be more willing to grant credit when they are trying to sell more vehicles. This is sometimes true in the early fall for the current year's models when the models for the next year are coming out.

You can watch several statistics ("barometers") that indicate that loans may become more available:

- The unemployment rate – When unemployment rates are below 5.5 percent, lenders may be more likely to make loans.

- The inflation rate – When inflation is below 3.0 percent, lenders are more confident that the money paid back will not have declined in value.

- Interest rates – Home mortgage rates below 7 percent are an indication of favorable lending conditions. Another interest rate that tracks the economy is the federal funds rate set by the Federal Reserve Board (the FED).

- Rate of growth in the economy – When the gross domestic product (GDP) is growing at 3.5 percent or more, the economy is strong and lenders are more willing to make loans.

By regularly reading newspaper articles on the economy you will become familiar with how the economy is doing. Many local newspapers focus on business-related topics on one particular day of the week—often Monday or Saturday. Reading the paper those days will help you understand credit conditions.

Use Collateral

Collateral refers to any asset you pledge to give up to the lender if you cannot make the debt payments as agreed. The asset is referred to as the "security" on the loan, and loans with collateral are referred to as secured loans. Collateral is very common on installment loans for homes and vehicles. People with little or no credit history can qualify for loans that they otherwise would not receive without collateral.

A car loan that is repaid in a timely fashion is one way to build good credit. Many car dealers will loan you money for cars regardless of your credit history, because the vehicle serves as collateral for the loan. But watch out for dealers who advertise heavily or focus primarily on those with no or poor credit history. They often charge steep interest rates. Their loan contracts often have terms that are very favorable for the lender and difficult to understand for someone new to using credit.

People who use secured loans to make purchases sometimes get carried away and finance more than they can afford. For example, vehicle values go down so rapidly that for most of the loan contract, the buyer is "upside down" in the loan (they owe more than the car is worth). Thus, they would have to come up with cash just to sell the vehicle.

Financing vehicles also builds a bad habit of making car payments. Once the vehicle is paid off, many consumers buy another car and start the cycle all over. As a result, they are never free of monthly payments. A better approach is to keep the vehicle well after the loan has been paid. When the loan payments end, put the money in the bank each month to save up for the next vehicle.

CAUTION: Don't use "I need to build credit" as an excuse to overspend on a car.

Lenders are more confident of repayment on secured loans. There is still some uncertainty, however. Lenders who repossess collateral sell it at an auction. Frequently the auction sale price is lower than the debt owed. This is very common on vehicle loans because of the "upside-down" problem describe above. People who take out loans with collateral should understand that if the collateral is not enough to cover the debt, they are still responsible for the remaining amount owed. This amount is referred to as a deficiency balance and is one reason why people should be very careful about using collateral.

There is one more way to offer more security to a lender and, thus, build your credit standing. This involves getting someone else who has a good credit reputation to promise to pay the debt if you cannot. Opening a joint credit card account can do this. A joint account builds credit histories in the names of both persons. Note, however, that each is responsible for the credit transactions carried out by the other. You can also get someone with a good credit history to cosign on your loan. This is commonly used when people with no credit history take out their first installment loan. Many people do this on their first vehicle loan.

Basically, opening a joint account or using a cosigner means that you have "borrowed" someone else's good credit reputation. This is a serious obligation. Your actions could end up harming both of your credit reputations. For this reason, many people are unwilling to be a cosigner for someone else.

Now, Back to Character

This discussion of capacity, capital, conditions and collateral is based on the idea that you can arrange things in certain ways to obtain credit more easily. To show that you have good credit character you then have to go ahead and get credit. At that point, your success or failure at building credit is up to you.

Credit card accounts generally do not build credit unless you actually use the card. This does not mean, however, that you have to carry a balance on a card to build credit. Pay your balance off each month. Similarly, you would never want to borrow money that you will have a tough time paying back just to build a credit history.

Think back again to your first job search. How did you build a good work experience? You did so by starting with a part-time job at a low wage. You worked hard and showed you could be trusted with greater and greater levels of responsibility. Eventually you moved up the ladder at your place of employment, or you got a better job somewhere else.

Building a good credit reputation is no different. You start small. You handle the responsibility well. You take on additional and more complicated debts and handle those well, too. Eventually, you will have a great credit reputation. Then you will qualify for credit at the lowest interest rates. And you will be able to borrow the amounts needed to reach major goals such as buying a home. Good luck!

What You Can Do!

Action Module 13: Building Credit When You Do Not Have Any

The Five C's of Credit can serve as a guide for building a good credit reputation when you do not have a credit history. This and earlier chapters provided specific information on how you can do so. The worksheets below can provide a way for you to list specific information or actions you can take related to the Five C's.

Action Module 13A | Five Steps I Can Take to Build My Credit CAPACITY

Having Sufficient Income to Pay Debts	
Step 1	
Step 2	
Step 3	
Step 4	
Step 5	

This worksheet is available for download at www.creditbooster.com/downloads/.

Action Module 13B | Five Steps I Can Take to Build My Credit CAPITAL

Borrower's Overall Level of Wealth and Assets	
Step 1	
Step 2	
Step 3	
Step 4	
Step 5	

This worksheet is available for download at www.creditbooster.com/downloads/.

Action Module 13C | Tracking Conditions Favorable for Borrowing

	Conditions Affecting Availability of Money to Lend
Step 1	
Step 2	
Step 3	
Step 4	
Step 5	

This worksheet is available for download at www.creditbooster com/downloads/.

Action Module 13D | Five Steps I Can Take to Build My Credit Collateral

	Items That Could be Used to Secure a Debt
Step 1	
Step 2	
Step 3	
Step 4	
Step 5	

This worksheet is available for download at www.creditbooster com/downloads/.

Action Module 13E | Five Steps I Can Take to Build My Credit CHARACTER

	Showing That I Can Handle Debt Responsibly
Step 1	
Step 2	
Step 3	
Step 4	
Step 5	

This worksheet is available for download at www.creditbooster.com/downloads/.

Summary

- Creditors treat no credit like bad credit.

- You can enhance your standing with possible lenders by increasing your capacity to pay back debt by taking steps to increase your income.

- Lenders will be more likely to loan money to people who have assets and for secured debts; those with collateral or a co-signer.

- Loans are easier to obtain during good economic times.

- Building your credit reputation generally requires that you obtain some type of credit and repay it as agreed. Start slowly and show you can handle debt responsibly.

We focused, in this chapter, on building credit when you don't have any as a special credit case. We continue in Chapter 14 on another special case—how divorce affects your credit. And in Chapter 15, we discuss another special case—how you can rebuild credit after bankruptcy.

Continuing on special case topics, we focus in this chapter on how divorce affects your credit and how you can rebuild your credit after divorce.

What You Need To Know!

When people marry they look forward to many years of emotional togetherness. Most married couples blend their financial lives, as well. When couples divorce, the emotional togetherness is broken. But the financial ties are often not as easily broken. In fact, the financial impacts of divorce can continue for many years.

If you are among those who may be facing divorce or who have recently gone through a divorce, you should be aware that divorce could have extremely adverse effects on your credit. Fortunately, there are some things you can do to avoid or minimize those consequences.

As in Chapter 13, we will use the 5 C's of credit to organize our discussion of divorce and your credit in this chapter. However, we will focus only on capacity, capital, and character. The other two C's—conditions and collateral—are not affected by divorce. You might want to look over those sections of Chapter 13 if you have not already done so.

The Effect of Divorce on Your "Credit Capacity"

Capacity refers to having sufficient income to afford the payments that would be required on a new loan or credit card account. Basically, lenders want to know if you can repay your debts. Judging your capacity includes comparing your income to your living expenses and the amount of debt you already have outstanding. Divorce affects both income and living expenses. It will also affect your ability to repay the debts for which you are responsible. Thus, divorce affects your credit capacity.

1. INCOME AND LIVING EXPENSES – Divorce will affect your income. Your personal income might go up if you take a part-time job or try to earn more money than you earn from the job you already have. But total household income is likely to decline because there is one fewer worker in the home. You will no longer have access to your partner's income in the same way as before. If you are receiving alimony or child support, these sources must be considered in your favor

by lenders when deciding to grant you credit. However, if those payments are not being received on a regular basis, lenders can consider that fact when they judge your credit worthiness.

Your day-to-day living expenses will also change after divorce. Whether they go up or down depends on which partner remains living in the marital home, child custody arrangements and whether alimony or child support must be paid or received. What is most likely is that the combined living expenses for both people will rise. That is because where there was one household there are now two.

2. **YOUR CURRENT DEBT** – Your level of debt after divorce will depend primarily on whose name or names were on the credit accounts you and your spouse had while married. There are three types of credit accounts: joint, individual, and authorized-user. Here are the key points you need to know about each type:

    -   Joint accounts. In a joint account, you and your ex-spouse BOTH are considered fully liable for the debt. Thus, lenders consider the entire debt to be your debt. This is true even if your ex-spouse was made responsible for the debt under your divorce decree. The impact of divorce decrees on debt is discussed below.

    -   Individual accounts. An individual account is exactly as it sounds. The named individual is solely responsible for the account. Thus, the lender cannot hold you responsible for your ex-spouse's individual accounts. Nor can the lender hold your ex-spouse responsible for your individual accounts.

    -   Authorized-user accounts. With an authorized-user account one party is the account holder and is responsible for the debt. However, the authorized user can use the account, usually with a credit card, without needing permission of the owner each time a transaction occurs. If you are an authorized-user on your ex-spouse's account, you will generally not be held responsible for the debt by the lender. As discussed below, the court might still hold you responsible under your divorce decree.

3. **THE IMPACT OF DIVORCE DECREES ON DEBTS OWED** – You should understand that the features of credit accounts are part of the contract between you and your ex-spouse and any credit grantors. Divorce decrees do not change these contracts. The divorce decree is not binding on the lender's contract with you and/or your ex-spouse.

In many divorce decrees, the court will make one of the parties responsible for a debt of the other or for their joint debts. Assume, for example, that a husband took out an individual loan to help pay for some educational expenses of the wife while she was in school. By contract, the debt is the husband's responsibility. However, in a divorce decree, the court might order the wife to repay the loan since she received the benefits of the education. Such orders, however, are not binding on the lender.

What this means is that should the wife fail to repay the money that the court ordered in the divorce decree, the husband will be held liable by the lender as stated under the original credit contract. The husband's only recourse would be to take the wife back to court to force her to pay him for amounts he paid on the loan. This can be a very difficult task. In the meantime, if the husband does not repay "his" legally obligated debt, the lender will pursue the usual collection procedures.

In community property states (Arizona, California, Idaho, Louisiana, Nevada, New Mexico, Texas, Washington, Wisconsin, and Puerto Rico), both spouses are considered co-responsible for any and all debts taken on while married, regardless of who is listed as the owner of the account. Thus, in community property states, you and your spouse are considered co-owners of all three types of accounts—individual credit accounts and authorized-user accounts and joint accounts. This means that if creditors cannot get repaid from one spouse, they will pursue the other person.

> **Warning: Sometimes divorce agreements stipulate that joint accounts may be maintained. This means that as long as your ex-spouse remains on the account, YOU will be liable for his or her future debts. If possible, try to avoid signing a divorce agreement that requires you to maintain a joint account with your ex-spouse. Listen to your attorney's advice on these matters.**

If your name must stay on a credit account, you will be legally liable for any new debts your ex-spouse runs up. It does not matter if your divorce agreement states that the account in question is solely your ex-spouse's responsibility. You are still legally liable to the lender; and if the ex-spouse should fail to pay, you will have to pay and then take action against the ex-spouse. Plus, if your ex-spouse is late in making payments, it will adversely affect your credit status, even if the problem resulted solely from your ex-spouse's actions. Now you should understand why it is so important to close all joint credit accounts.

> **If your ex-spouse is ordered to pay off a joint credit card debt, it might be a good idea to continue to pay at least he minimum payment to protect your own credit.**

Credit card accounts are open-ended and, thus, can remain open for decades even if you never have or no longer use the card. Accounts are not closed if you cut up the cards. The lender must be formally notified of your request.

Here's what to do:

1. Obtain the customer-service telephone number for the lender from your most recent monthly statement or your credit report.

2. Contact the lender to request the address to use when sending a cancellation request. This will not be same address that is used to send your monthly payment.

3. Send a written request to close the account and request that the creditor send a confirmation that the account is closed.

4. After 90 days obtain a copy of your credit reports from each of the three major national credit bureaus to ensure that the account is shown as closed.

Note, that you cannot "close" an account on which you currently owe a balance. However, you can ask the lender to no longer honor the card.

The Effect of Divorce on Your "Credit Capital"

Capital refers to your overall level of wealth. A lender wants to know that you have sufficient financial assets if they are needed to repay the debt. Basically, they want to know what you own.

Some assets are owned individually. They are owned solely in your name. An example is a checking account that only you can use. Most people own cars individually.

Married couples often own many assets jointly. These can include their homes as well as their checking and savings accounts. In community property states, virtually all assets are treated by the courts as if it were jointly owned.

1. FORMS OF JOINT OWNERSHIP

- Joint tenancy with right of survivorship (also called joint tenancy) is the most common form of joint ownership, especially for husbands and wives. In this case, each person owns the whole of the asset and can dispose of it without the approval of the other(s). When an owner dies, his or her share is divided equally among the other owners. An advantage of this form of ownership while married is the ease of access for each owner. This advantage becomes a disadvantage after a divorce because one person can withdraw all of the money in the joint account without the other's knowledge.

- Tenancy in common is a form of joint ownership in which two or more parties own the asset, but each owns a separate share. In most states, the ownership shares are presumed to be equal unless otherwise specified. One owner cannot sell the entire asset but potentially sell his or her share. When one owner dies his or her share in the asset is distributed according to the terms of a will (or, if no will exists, according to state law) instead of automatically going to the other co-owner(s).

- Tenancy by the entirety, which exists in about 30 states, is restricted to property held between a husband and a wife. Under this arrangement, no one co-owner can sell or dispose of his or her portion of an asset without the permission of the other. This type of account provides the tightest control over checking or savings because both signatures are required for checks or withdrawal slips. This restriction effectively prevents withdrawals by one owner without the knowledge of the other.

2. **MARITAL VERSUS NON-MARITAL PROPERTY** – One big question that arises in divorce relates to the rights a non-owner spouse has in the individually owned property of the other spouse. Individually owned property is generally divided into marital property and non-marital property.

One form of **non-marital property** is property owned by the spouse before the marriage. For example, one spouse may have owned a vehicle when the marriage took place. This would be non-marital property. To change that status, the other spouse's name would have to be put on the title to the vehicle. The second major type of non-marital property is the gifts and inheritances received individually by one of the spouses during the marriage even if the other spouse gave the gift. A spouse has no ownership rights in the non-marital property owned by the other. Thus, non-marital property can serve as credit "capital" for the ex-spouse who owns it. For example, if one spouse received a vehicle as a gift from his or her parent, that vehicle would serve as an asset for the receiving spouse.

Marital property consists of property acquired by the couple during the marriage even if it is owned individually by one spouse. An example might be the furniture in their home. Even if the husband purchased the furniture out of funds from his own checking account or by using his own individual credit card, the property is considered to be marital property. In community property states, almost all of the money and property acquired during a marriage is legally considered the joint property of both spouses and, thus, is marital property.

It is the marital property that divorcing spouses often fight about in a divorce. The division of marital property typically is outlined in the divorce decree issued by the court. As with debts, the divorce decree is binding on the ex-spouses but not necessarily binding on a bank, credit union, or vehicle-financing company where an account is held. For example, a divorce decree might state that a jointly owned savings account be awarded to one spouse. To accomplish this, the formal ownership documents must be changed with the bank. Similarly, if one spouse is awarded ownership of the couple's home, the deed must be changed to reflect this ruling.

The Effect of Divorce on Your "Credit Character"

Your credit character refers to your credit reputation as contained in your credit report. Justifiably or not, your credit reputation is tied to that of your spouse. All of your joint credit experience while married is part of your credit report. Your spouse may have had considerable individual credit in his or her name. If that experience was positive, it will no longer be of any help in your newly divorced credit experience. If you were a spouse who did not have credit accounts in your own name (or jointly), it could mean that you have no credit history at all! Your first step should be to request copies of your individual credit reports from all three national credit reporting agencies (see Chapter 5). If the reports indicate no past credit usage in your name, you can use the information in Chapter 13 to begin to build your own credit history.

What You Can Do!

Action Module 14: Building Credit After Divorce

Building and maintaining good credit after divorce can be challenging because income is usually lower and the costs and disruptions of divorce often add to both spouses' overall debt load. But it is not impossible. The key to an excellent credit status is to take the right actions in each of the three areas most likely to be affected by divorce: capacity, capital and character.

1. **MAINTAINING YOUR "CREDIT CAPACITY" AFTER DIVORCE** – There are a number of steps you can take to make sure that lenders rate your credit "capacity" as highly as possible after divorce:

   - Keep track of every dollar you earn and spend for a month or two after your divorce. Then develop an income and expense statement for each month (See Chapter 3). This will let you visualize your new income and spending patterns now that you are divorced. If you are not yet divorced, try to make estimates based on what you expect your income and expenses to be.

   - Develop a budget and stick to it as best as you can (See Chapter 8). In your budget, set aside savings for an emergency fund that should grow over time to at least two or three times your monthly expenses. This fund will help you weather or survive unexpected expenses.

   - If you have a balance owed on a joint credit account and cannot pay it off before or soon after the divorce, write the creditor. Ask that the account be officially "closed." Also ask that the balance owed be transferred into an individual account of the spouse who has agreed to be responsible (or was required to by the divorce decree) for that particular debt. Be certain to ask the creditor to send you a letter confirming that the old joint account has been closed.

- Also, have your ex-spouse removed as an authorized user on all of your credit accounts. If necessary, you might want to close these accounts and have the lenders move any balances to new, individual accounts in your name. Again, be certain to obtain written confirmation from lenders that the old accounts have been closed.

> **If needed, ask your attorney to help you change the ownership of all credit accounts to fit the provisions of your divorce decree.**

To get started on these tasks, you can use the **Debt Inventory Worksheet** below. It is very similar to the worksheet in **Action Module 1A** in Chapter 1. Two additional columns are added: Spouse Responsible in Divorce Decree so that you can record who is responsible for the debt under your divorce decree and Action To Take to indicate the action you wish to take regarding closing or maintaining the account.

Action Module 14A | My New Debt Inventory

Account	Type of Account	Spouse Responsible in Divorce Decree	Balance	Monthly Payment	Action to Take
Example: Togs for Tots Credit Card	*Joint*	*Me*	*$1000*	*Varies*	*Keep as joint account but pay $150 per month to pay off one year and then close account*

This worksheet is available for download at www.creditbooster.com/downloads/.

2. **MAINTAINING YOUR "CREDIT CAPITAL" AFTER DIVORCE** – There are a number of steps you can take to make sure that lenders rate you as highly as possible for "capital" after divorce:

- Develop a list of all your assets—monetary, tangible and investment (see Chapter 2). Then identify how those assets are owned and their current fair market values.

- Make certain that all of your non-marital property is properly listed in your name.

- Review your divorce decree and have the ownership legally changed on any property that was awarded to you, such as a vehicle or television.

To get started on these tasks you can use these *Action Modules 14B*, *14C* and *14D Worksheets*.

Action Module 14B │ My Asset Ownership Worksheet - Monetary

Account	How Owned?	Current Value	Action to Take
Example: Checking Account	*Joint*	*$1200*	*Close the account and open separate individual accounts-$600 each*

This worksheet is available for download at www.creditbooster.com/downloads/

Action Module 14C | My Asset Ownership Worksheet - Tangible

Tangible Asset	How Owned?	Current Value	Action to Take

This worksheet is available for download at www.creditbooster.com/downloads/

Action Module 14D | My Asset Ownership Worksheet - Investment

Investment Asset	How Owned?	Current Value	Action to Take

This worksheet is available for download at www.creditbooster.com/downloads/

3. MAINTAINING YOUR "CREDIT CHARACTER" AFTER DIVORCE – After divorce your credit character as measured by your credit bureaus files will still be tied to your ex-spouse in two important ways. First, all your past credit behaviors will remain as part of your personal credit history. Secondly, all future credit behaviors in any joint accounts will continue to affect both your credit histories. You cannot do anything about the past. But you can ensure that your future credit information is based solely on your own credit behavior. The actions you should take will differ depending on your current credit status:

- If You Currently Have Good Credit – If you and your ex-spouse (or soon-to-be ex-spouse) have good credit, you should close all joint accounts. Ask creditors to transfer the balances to the appropriate individual accounts, as the two of you decided.

- If You Currently Have No Credit – You may have no credit history at all if all accounts were solely in your ex-spouses name or if you were only an authorized-user on the accounts. Having no credit history could make it extremely difficult to obtain credit at a time when you are financially vulnerable and may need access to credit. You should contact each of the three big credit bureaus and request that they begin a new file solely in your name. You should then use the steps outlined in Chapter 13 to build your own good credit reputation.

- If You Have Poor Credit – Sadly, you may have bad credit through no fault of your own. You may be able to challenge entries in your credit history that really should have been only in your ex-spouse's history. Chapters 5, 6, 9 and 10 of **CreditBooster**™ provide information and suggested actions to take to address a poor credit history and improve your credit scores.

If your ex-spouse creates new bad debt in a joint account, contact your divorce attorney to see if you have any legal recourse. If your spouse runs up huge debts in a joint account and creditors come after you, one recourse could be bankruptcy. Listen to the advice of your attorney on these matters.

> **If a divorce is pending and your spouse has bad credit, contact your divorce attorney for advice.**

If either spouse declares bankruptcy, it will not wipe out or eliminate alimony, maintenance, or child support payments owed to you (or by you). If you fear that your former spouse is going to file for bankruptcy, you need to contact your divorce attorney immediately to learn how to protect your credit and your finances.

Even if a divorce is final, you can still take steps to rebuild your credit. What steps will you take in the next 24 hours to start rebuilding poor credit as a result of divorce? Use *Action Module 14E Worksheet* as a resource.

Action Module 14E | Building Credit Character Worksheet

(Example: I will order my individual credit reports online to review them immediately.)

1. _____

2. _____

3. _____

4. _____

5. _____

6. _____

7. _____

8. _____

This worksheet is available for download at www.creditbooster.com/downloads/.

Summary

- Any negative information from joint accounts affects the credit history of both spouses.

- If you are an authorized-user on your spouse's account, you may have no credit history at all. Request copies of your individual credit report to find out.

- In community property states, you and your spouse are considered co-owners of all debts, regardless of whose name is on the account.

- In case of divorce, close all joint accounts.

- You are still liable for your spouse's debt in joint accounts, regardless of what the divorce degree says. If you spouse fails to pay a debt as ordered in a divorce decree, you will have to pay the debt to protect your credit history. You should then contact your attorney to take action against your ex-spouse to force payment to you.

- If you fear that your former spouse is going to file for bankruptcy, contact your divorce attorney immediately to protect your credit and finances.

In this section we have focused on the Special Cases of building credit when you don't have any as a special credit case and how to build your "credit" capacity in the face of divorce. In Chapter 15, we will discuss a last special case—how you can rebuild credit after bankruptcy.

This chapter examines various factors that relate to post-bankruptcy credit management. If you have filed for bankruptcy protection, this information will highlight the appropriate decisions and steps you may have to take now and in the future.

What You Need To Know!

Filing for Bankruptcy

Filing for bankruptcy is a means provided to deal with your debt problems. When a person goes through bankruptcy he or she is basically asking the court to forgive a portion of his or her debts. If the judge approves, the debts forgiven are said to be **discharged** and will no longer be owed. Bankruptcy may allow a person to erase many, but not necessarily all, debts and start over.

> **DEFINITION: Bankruptcy is a court action that can eliminate many of your debts, stop creditors from calling you, and give you a new start financially.**

Bankruptcy offers some resolution to your financial worries. However, it also carries negative consequences and major responsibilities that you will have to assume, so you can conduct your post-bankruptcy financial affairs in a positive direction.

Rebuilding Credit after Bankruptcy

There are two types of bankruptcy. Chapter 7 Bankruptcy calls for the sale of most of your assets with the proceeds of the sale applied to your debts. The remaining debt is discharged. Chapter 13 Bankruptcy establishes a five-year, court-approved plan for you to pay a portion of your debts. If you complete the plan, the remaining debt is discharged. Persons whose income is below the median income for their state may choose Chapter 7 or Chapter 13. Others must use Chapter 13 even if they can afford to pay as little $100 per month towards their debts.

Many consumers think that if they declare bankruptcy, they can never get credit again. The fact is that the history of a bankruptcy will stay in one's credit bureau files for ten years. Also, once a person has filed for Chapter 7 Bankruptcy he or she is prohibited from declaring bankruptcy again for eight years.

Some lenders specialize in providing credit to consumers with prior bankruptcies. Those companies figure that if a person has just declared bankruptcy and has steady employment, he is likely to be able to handle repaying on a few new debts. These lenders know that this person is prohibited from declaring Chapter 7 Bankruptcy again for eight years.

Soon after a bankruptcy discharge, many bankrupts start to receive offers for new credit cards. Sometimes auto dealers who specialize in used cars target recent bankrupts who may have lost their vehicle through the bankruptcy process. Note, however, that the interest rates on these sources of credit are extremely high—24 to 30 percent is common.

If you take the proper steps after declaring bankruptcy and also manage your credit responsibly, you can rebuild an improved credit reputation in a few years. Studies show that 18 to 24 months after discharge of bankruptcy, most consumers can qualify for a home mortgage with terms just as good as consumers with the same financial characteristics who have not filed for bankruptcy.

Bankruptcy and Your Five "C"s of Credit

As in Chapter 13, we will use the five C's of credit to organize our discussion of bankruptcy and your credit in this chapter. We will focus on capacity, capital, collateral and character. The last of the 5 C's—conditions—is not affected by bankruptcy.

THE EFFECT OF BANKRUPTCY ON YOUR "CREDIT CAPACITY"

Capacity refers to having sufficient income to afford the payments that would be required on a new loan or credit card account. Basically, lenders want to know if you can afford to repay your debts. Judging your capacity includes comparing your income to your living expenses and to the amount of debt you already have outstanding. Bankruptcy clearly affects the amount of debt you have outstanding. In a very real sense, bankruptcy improves your credit capacity because your debts are reduced.

Before bankruptcy, most debtors have higher monthly debt repayment obligations than they could handle. The pressure to make those payments is often the major reason why people consider bankruptcy. But, after bankruptcy, most debt is gone. Thus, certain ratios such as the debt payments-to-take home pay and debt service-to-gross income (see Chapter 4) actually look better to lenders.

Do not forget that some debts cannot be absolved through bankruptcy. Such debts include income taxes, child support or alimony, and debts for personal injuries you caused while driving under the influence of drugs or alcohol. Debtors with a high level of such debt may not see much of an impact on their credit capacity after bankruptcy. Non-discharged debts will need to be repaid as originally agreed and one's monthly payments may not change.

Finally, there is another type of debt that may continue after bankruptcy. There are certain assets in bankruptcy that are exempt from seizure by the courts. Your principal home is an example. Depending on your state's bankruptcy laws, you may be able to keep a specified dollar amount of equity in that home, and also an inexpensive vehicle and tools you need to use on your job. But what if you still owe money on a loan used to buy these assets. Would the court require that you turn over the asset to pay a portion of the debt? Possibly not.

For example, perhaps you own a vehicle worth $5000 based on its replacement cost at its age and condition, but on which you still owe $2600. Assume that you live in a state where you are allowed to keep up to $3000 value in a vehicle. In this case, the value of the vehicle qualifies for the exemption because the ownership equity in the vehicle is less than $3000 ($5000-$2600 = $2400). But, what about the debt owed on the vehicle? Under Chapter 7 Bankruptcy, you must pay the remaining debt in a lump-sum during your bankruptcy process. Under Chapter 13, you may be able to reaffirm this debt with the lender and repay the full amount through your Plan.

THE EFFECT OF BANKRUPTCY ON YOUR "CREDIT CAPITAL"

Capital refers to your overall level of wealth. A lender wants to know that you have sufficient financial assets should they be needed to repay the debt. Basically, the lender wants to know what you own.

Bankruptcy affects your credit capital, but the effect depends on the type of bankruptcy you chose and the type of assets you owned.

Under Chapter 7 Bankruptcy, many of the debtor's assets are turned over to the court to pay some of the debt owed. Any money in a checking or savings account can be taken by the court. Also, a person's investments may be liquidated. Some tangible assets are sold. The result can be a much lower overall roster of assets for the debtor. Depending on your state, however, you might be allowed to keep certain assets, such as a portion of the equity in your home, a vehicle, and a certain amount of personal property. Thus, your assets may not decline as much as you might think, thereby maintaining after bankruptcy a level of credit capital relatively comparable to that before bankruptcy. The particulars in your state may be obtained from an attorney who specializes in bankruptcy.

Chapter 13 Bankruptcy focuses on the income of the debtor. The court sets up a plan to pay as much as possible on the debts owed, given the level of income of the debtor. This form of bankruptcy can allow the debtor to keep assets after bankruptcy as long as the debt payment plan set up by the courts is followed. Thus, credit capital may be largely unchanged by Chapter 13 Bankruptcy.

For more information on Chapter 7 and Chapter 13 Bankruptcy, visit the InCharge® Education Foundation's Debtor Education Web site at www.personalfinanceeducation.com.

THE EFFECT OF BANKRUPTCY ON YOUR "CREDIT COLLATERAL"

Collateral refers to assets that could be or are pledged as security on a debt. In most situations, if a person misses a few payments on an asset pledged as security, like a car or TV set, the lender takes legal action to repossess it. After Chapter 7 Bankruptcy, debtors usually have few assets that could be used as collateral. That is because they were taken by the court and used to pay a portion of the debts owed.

But this situation is only temporary. Two factors can lead to improved access to collateral after bankruptcy:

1. The former debtor can build a savings account that can be used as collateral. After bankruptcy the debtor may find that he can begin a regular savings program and accumulate funds in a savings account. This is because debt payments will no longer be such a large part of the former debtor's budget. These funds may be able to be used as collateral on a debt; especially a secured credit card.

   A **secured credit card** is a credit card backed by a savings account opened at the financial institution that issues the card. The savings account serves as collateral for the card. The credit limit on the card will be from 50 to 200 percent the amount in the account. So, perhaps a $1000 deposit will secure a credit card with a limit of $500 (50%) to $2000 (200%). Generally, the amount in the savings account cannot be touched as long as the credit card account is open. If one does not repay on the secured credit card, the card issuer can take your savings as it "secures" your credit account.

You should be wary of certain aspects of secured cards:

- Some secured cards will have a very high application fee, perhaps $200. One can shop around for a lower fee.

- If a person wants a high credit limit on a secured card, he or she will have to deposit much more money into the savings account.

- With some secured cards, the issuer establishes the savings account by taking a cash advance against the credit card and then starts charging the minimum monthly fee that includes the interest on the card.

Consider this example. Jana Parsons is offered a secured card with a limit of $4000, at an interest rate of 24 percent (2% per month). The minimum payment per month is 3 percent of the balance on the card. She can take a cash advance of $4000 against the card to set up the savings account. At first, she will not be able to use the card because the balance and the credit limit are the same. But eventually she can start using the card as she pays down the balance. This offer emphasizes the benefits of the card in rebuilding Jana's credit.

In reality, this is how the offer really works. Her first month's bill would have a $120 minimum payment (3% x $4000), of which $80 is interest (2% x $4000). This means that she would pay only $40 ($120 - $80) on the $4000 if she made the minimum payment. At that rate it would be several years before she would have access to any meaningful borrowing capacity on the card. The lender, of course, benefits greatly from this arrangement.

> **TIP: You should avoid any secured card that uses a cash advance to establish the savings account deposit.**

Bankrupts should shop very carefully for secured credit cards and read the rules and fees on the card very closely. *Action Module 15C* below provides a worksheet that can be used to shop for secured credit cards after bankruptcy.

2. The former debtor might take out a loan to buy an item that can serve as collateral on the loan. Because of the former debtor's improved budget situation, the person can "afford" to make some debt payments should he want to borrow money. Lenders know this and many are willing to make loans to bankrupts provided there is sufficient collateral for the loan.

For example, assume that Peter Arnell has recently been through bankruptcy. He would like to purchase a more reliable vehicle but is worried that he could not obtain a loan. He has saved up about $2000 and thinks he could afford a monthly payment of up to $250. He could borrow up to about $6000 for $230 per month at 22 percent. (His rate might be this high because of his bankruptcy. Adding in his $2000 he might be able to purchase an $8000 vehicle.) His down payment would be 25 percent ($2000/$8000). The lender would feel confident that the vehicle holds enough value to pay the loan if repossession becomes necessary.

Persons who have gone through bankruptcy need to be very cautious about entering into loan agreements to purchase vehicles. This is especially true if the lender is one who targets lending to people with "bad credit" or who uses a "Buy Here—Pay Here" approach. The most important negative is that these loans will charge a very high interest rate. A second disadvantage is that some of the terms of these loans can be really unfair. For example, in some cases the title of the vehicle is not transferred to the buyer until the last payment is made. This makes repossession very easy. Third, most of these loans have very strict rules about late payments so that being even one day late might mean a steep late payment fee, perhaps $100. And sometimes a fee, such as $25, might even be charged per day. Then it will quickly escalate into an unaffordable amount.

In some cases, the loan contract is written in such a way that it almost guarantees that the borrower will be unable to pay (e.g., through rapidly escalating late fees) and the vehicle will be repossessed. Many of these lenders prey upon people who previously declared bankruptcy and who may have no other access to credit. Bankrupts should shop very carefully for loans and read the entire contract. *Action Module 15D* below provides a worksheet that can be used to shop for loans after bankruptcy.

THE EFFECT OF BANKRUPTCY ON YOUR "CREDIT CHARACTER"

Your credit character is the last of the 5 C's of credit but is the one most affected by bankruptcy. Lenders will be very cautious in the future about granting credit to you. They will not take into account any of your valid reasons for the bankruptcy. They will only see that it occurred.

You might ask if you will ever be trusted again when it comes to credit. Fortunately, the answer is yes. But it will take some time and certainly some effort and careful financial management on your part.

The impact of bankruptcy will clearly be seen in your credit score. As discussed in Chapter 5, credit scores have a big impact on the availability of credit and the interest rate paid to get credit. Thus, it is wise to do all you can to rebuild your credit after bankruptcy. The section below describes the actions you can take to do just that.

What You Can Do!

Action Module 15: Building Credit after Bankruptcy

You probably want to rebuild your credit as soon as possible. There are some steps that can help speed up the process. The key to obtaining an excellent credit status is to take the right actions in each of the four areas most likely to be affected by bankruptcy: Capacity, Capital, Collateral and Character.

Maintaining Your "Credit Capacity" after Bankruptcy

There are a number of steps you can take to make sure that lenders rate you as highly as possible for "capacity" after bankruptcy:

- KEEP TRACK OF EVERY DOLLAR YOU EARN AND SPEND FOR A MONTH OR TWO AFTER YOUR BANKRUPTCY – Then develop an income and expense statement for each month (See Chapter 3). This will let you visualize your new income and spending patterns now that you are bankrupt. If you are not yet bankrupt, try to make estimates based on what you expect your income and expenses to be.

- DEVELOP A BUDGET AND STICK TO IT AS BEST AS YOU CAN (See Chapter 8) – In your budget, set aside savings for an emergency fund that should grow over time to at least two or three times your monthly expenses. This fund will help you weather or survive unexpected expenses.

- IN YOUR BUDGET YOU WILL NEED TO TAKE SPECIAL CARE TO PAY ON TIME, IN FULL, EVERY MONTH ANY DEBTS YOU STILL OWE AFTER BANKRUPTCY – This is especially true for reaffirmed debts. Failure to make a payment as required can mean immediate repossession of the asset and another negative entry in your credit bureau files.

To get started on these tasks you can use the **Action Module 15A: My Debts after Bankruptcy Worksheet** below. It is very similar to the worksheet in **Action Module 1A** in Chapter 1. Once you have a listing of all your debts, you should include them in your budget.

Action Module 15A | My Debts After Bankruptcy

Account	Limit or Original Amount Borrowed	APR	Balance	Payoff Date (in months)	Monthly Payment*	Comments
Example: Reaffirmed Auto Loan	*$4000*	*9%*	*$2600*	*36*	*$82.68*	*Hope to pay off early.*
TOTAL		n/a				

This worksheet is available for download at www.creditbooster.com/downloads/

*See **Table 1** in Chapter 1 to determine the monthly payment needed to pay off your debts within the time period desired.*

Maintaining Your "Credit Capital" after Bankruptcy

There are a number of steps you can take to make sure that lenders rate you as highly as possible for "capital" after bankruptcy:

- Update your list of assets: Monetary, Tangible, and Investment (see Chapter 2)

- Identify assets that might serve as collateral should you need to use credit

- Make provision in your budget to build monetary assets and investment assets using the "pay yourself first" philosophy.

To get started on these tasks you can use *Action Module 15B: My Asset Worksheet*. Even if you do not intend to use any of your assets as collateral on a loan, filling out the worksheet is a good idea because your asset mix is usually different after bankruptcy.

Action Module 15B | My Asset Worksheet

Asset	Current Value	Could Be Used As Collateral Should Credit Be Needed?
Example: Savings Account	*$3000*	*Could be used to obtain a secured credit card.*

This worksheet is available for download at www.creditbooster.com/downloads/

Building/Using Your "Credit Collateral" after Bankruptcy

Unsecured credit is difficult to obtain after bankruptcy. Access to secured loans is often still available (but at high interest rates). Secured loans are often backed up by collateral. Examples are secured credit cards and vehicle loans. But these sources of credit can be very expensive. Plus, the contracts contain requirements or features that put the borrower at risk for high fees. They also add to the likelihood of nonpayment, thereby adding to an already negative credit status.

Action Module 15C: Comparing Secured Credit Card Offers provides a way to compare several different secured credit card offers. Once you have gathered information from perhaps three sources, you can compare the information available there to the information on secured cards provided earlier in this chapter.

Action Module 15C | Comparing Secured Credit Card Offers

Card Feature	Example: Town Bank Secured Credit Card	Card #1	Card #2	Card #3	Card #4
Credit Limit	$2000				
Deposit Required	$2000				
How is Deposit to be Paid	Cash				
Initial Sign-up Fee	$300				
Credit Card APR for Purchases	21.00%				
Credit Card APR for Balance Transfers	24.99%				
Credit Card APR for Cash Advances	24.99%				
Default Rate	27.99%				
Variable or Fixed Rate	Variable				
If APR is Variable, How Calculated	Prime plus 13% for purchases; prime plus 16% for transfers and cash advances; prime pluss 22% for default rate				
Grace Period for Repayment of Credit Card Purchases	None				

(continued)

(continued)

Card Feature	Example: Town Bank Secured Credit Card	Card #1	Card #2	Card #3	Card #4
Grace Period for Credit Card Cash Advances and Balance Transfers	*None*				
Method of Computing the Balance	*Average Daily Balance (including new purchases)*				
Annual Fee	*$70*				
Minimum Finance Charge	*$5*				
Transaction Fee for Credit Card Cash Advances and Balance Transfers	*The higher of $50 or 5%*				
Bounced Payment Check Fee	*$100*				
Late Fee	*$70 on balances up to $500, $100 on balances over $500*				
Credit Card Over the Limit Fee	*None*				

This worksheet is available for download at www.creditbooster.com/downloads/

Action Module 15D: Vehicle Loan Worksheet provides a handy way to compare among several different or vehicle loan offers.

Action Module 15D | Vehicle Loan Worksheet

Loan Feature	Example: We Make It Easy Auto Log	Card #1	Card #2	Card #3	Card #4
Make and model of vehicle	1995 Totota Corolla				
Purchase price	$8000				
Trade-in	None				
Amount to be borrowed	$6000				
APR for loan	21%				
Number of months	36				
Monthly payment	$230				
Variable or fixed rate	Fixed				
Application fee	$100				
Monthly processing fee	$25				
Bounced check fee	$50				
Late fee	$20 per day				

This worksheet is available for download at www.creditbooster.com/downloads/.

Maintaining Your "Credit Character" after Bankruptcy

After bankruptcy, your credit character as measured by your credit bureaus files will be very poor. All your past negative credit behaviors will remain as part of your personal credit history. You cannot do anything about the past, but you can take steps to ensure that your future credit information will be based on good credit behavior.

Sadly, you may have been forced into bankruptcy through no real fault of your own. Examples are medical bills, divorce, and unemployment. But bankruptcy does give you a fresh start. And now you are in control of your financial life. You may feel that you never want to borrow money again. That is not such a bad idea. But in today's world it may not always be realistic. Credit cards are needed by travelers when making reservations and for emergencies, for example.

Once a bankruptcy is final, you can begin to take steps to rebuild your credit. What will you take in the next days and months to start rebuilding poor credit as a result of bankruptcy? Use *Action Module 15E: Building Credit Character Worksheet* as a tool.

Action Module 15E | Building Credit Character Worksheet

Steps to be taken.

[Sample] I will order my individual credit reports online to review them immediately.
[Sample] I will repay my remaining debt on-time, in-full, every month.

1. _____

2. _____

3. _____

4. _____

5. _____

6. _____

7. _____

8. _____

9. _____

10. _____
This worksheet is available for download at www.creditbooster.com/downloads/.

Summary

- If you take the proper steps after declaring bankruptcy and also manage your credit responsibly, you can rebuild an improved credit reputation in a few years.

- In rebuilding your credit, it is helpful to focus on the following four "C"s of credit: Capacity, Capital, Collateral, and Character.

- Capacity refers to having sufficient income to afford the payments that would be required on a new loan or credit card account. After bankruptcy, most debt is gone. In a very real sense, bankruptcy improves your credit capacity because your debts are reduced.

- Capital refers to your overall level of wealth. A lender wants to know that you have sufficient financial assets should they be needed to repay the debt. Basically, the lender wants to know what you own. Bankruptcy affects your credit capital, but the effect depends on the type of bankruptcy you chose and the type of assets you owned.

- Collateral refers to assets that could be or are pledged as security on a debt. After Chapter 7 Bankruptcy, debtors usually have few assets that could be used as collateral. That is because they were taken by the court and used to pay a portion of the debts owed. Steps that can be taken include:
  - The former debtor can build a savings account that can be used as collateral
  - The former debtor might take out a loan to buy an item that can serve as collateral on the loan.

- Your credit character is the last of the 5 C's of credit but is the one most affected by bankruptcy. Lenders will be very cautious in the future about granting credit to you. They will not take into account any of your valid reasons for the bankruptcy. They will only see that it occurred. You might ask if you will ever be trusted again when it comes to credit. Fortunately, the answer is yes. But it will take some time and certainly some effort and careful financial management on your part.

- After bankruptcy, you can rebuild credit in the following ways among others:
  - Set up a budget that provides for repayment of your remaining debts and the building of assets.
  - Keep an existing credit card by reaffirming the debt.
  - Getting a secured credit card or vehicle loan but only if it is affordable and the contract is fair to you the borrower.
  - Do not take on any new debt unless you are absolutely positive that you can repay as agreed.

Rebuilding your credit reputation is important and doable. You can succeed by starting small. You can handle credit again. Over time, you will regain your good credit reputation. Your capacity for credit will be high. You will have the capital needed to obtain low cost credit. You will be able to obtain credit on your own good name and not rely solely on collateral to obtain credit. And your credit character as measured by your credit reports and your credit scores will again be positive. Then you will qualify for credit at lower interest rates. **Good luck!**

Conclusion

The end of this book is really just the beginning of your journey toward a lifetime of better credit. The key thing to know and understand is that your credit profile is fluid. Credit scores are not etched in stone, so even someone with excellent credit today must maintain good credit and debt management habits on a regular basis or risk seeing their credit score and credit worthiness diminish.

The idea is not to fear the lending and credit industries but to understand, through this book and others, how the industries keep score so as you play the financial ball park, you'll know and understand the rules and what it takes to be a winner. It is not always easy to keep doing the right things financially all the time. There are may opportunities that we confront as consumers to stray back toward using debt to finance a lifestyle we cannot afford.

Life will have its ups and downs financially so it would be foolish to think anyone could go a lifetime without credit challenges at some point. Many things happen that are out of our control so the best strategy as consumers is to work to prepare ourselves using good financial times to set a strong foundation that will carry us through any unforeseen difficulties in the future.

CreditBooster™ provides a framework for you to build, re-build, or maintain your credit status in order to gain the maximum credit worthiness and benefits from excellent credit reports and scores. You now know what is important in the development and ongoing reporting of your credit activity. You should feel confident in using this tool to aggressively manage your credit and other financial activities in a way that gives you the best possible outcome.

We thank you for the opportunity to pass this important knowledge on to you and your family and encourage you to continue to seek out, learn, and practice smart personal finance strategies.

Helpful Resources

InCharge® Debt Solutions

IN CHARGE·
DEBT SOLUTIONS

Are you struggling with credit card and other personal debts?

Are you falling behind on your bills? Are collectors calling you at home? At work? InCharge® Debt Solutions can help you.

At InCharge® Debt Solutions, our certified counselors will work one-on-one with you to analyze your financial situation and provide a proper solution that best meets your needs. If the Debt Management Program is recommended our certified counselors will stay in close contact with you to ensure you receive the support necessary to be successful on the program. Every InCharge® counselor must receive accreditation through the Association for Financial Counseling and Planning Education (AFCPE), an independent certification provider. In addition to personalized counseling, you will receive specialized communications, including newsletters, e-mails and educational products, all designed to update, educate, and motivate. All communications are completely confidential and discreet to ensure your privacy.

Professional. Personal. Private. At InCharge® Debt Solutions, our certified counselors will work one-on-one with you to provide the personalized attention necessary to find a solution that meets your needs. If a Debt Management Program (DMP) is recommended, a Personal Care Counselor will be assigned to your account and will serve as your primary contact during the first three to six months. Our counselors take a proactive role, staying in close contact to ensure you receive the support necessary to be successful on the program. Every InCharge® counselor must receive accreditation through the Association for Financial Counseling and Planning Education (AFCPE), an independent certification provider. In addition to personalized counseling, you will benefit throughout the term of your DMP from specialized communications, including newsletters, e-mails and educational products, all designed to update, educate, and motivate. All communications are completely confidential and discreet to ensure your privacy.

Solutions-Based Approach. We recognize that Debt Management Programs are not the answer for everyone. For individuals we feel would not qualify for or benefit from a DMP, we provide financial counseling, which includes budget assistance, money management education and, if applicable, referrals to social service agencies or partners that can help with mortgage problems or student loans.

The result: in many cases your counselor can complete a proactive counseling session in one call and provide immediate relief—something few, if any, or our competitors can promise! Benefits that last a lifetime. The benefits of InCharge® Debt Solutions continue long after your initial counseling session, regardless of whether or not you enroll in our Debt Management Program. Our counseling and educational services help you develop a long-term plan for managing your finances. Through our web portal, www.incharge.org, and through personal finance publications like *Next Step: A Monthly Guide to Reaching Your Financial Goals* and *Your Money: A Guide to Managing Your Credit and Debt*, we address issues such as budgeting, managing cash flow, understanding credit reports, using credit effectively and avoiding bankruptcy. With our help, you won't just get out of debt— you'll have the tools you need to stay out of debt.

Sound Business Practices. InCharge® is dedicated to providing the highest level of quality and operates under the most stringent of professional guidelines. As part of our commitment to excellence, InCharge® undergoes independent audits, is certified under the ISO 9001:2000 standard, and is a member of the Association of Independent Consumer Credit Counseling Agencies (AICCCA).

Get help today by speaking to an InCharge® Credit Counselor in confidence: 1-866-254-8925 or visit www.incharge.org.

More InCharge® Education

InCharge® Education Foundation, Inc is led by a dedicated staff of experts in the fields of personal finance education and research, the InCharge® Education Foundation Inc. is nationally recognized for reaching out to consumers with engaging educational programs and products. These include:

YOUNG MONEY

YOUNG MONEY® Magazine, which skillfully delivers to its 18-to-24-year-old audience a unique blend of money, business and lifestyle topics that engages, informs and inspires. A recognized brand at major college campuses across the country, each issue of YOUNG MONEY® magazine is read bi-monthly by more than 750,000 young adults. Over one million people have visited www.youngmoney.com and thousands of college students have participated in YOUNG MONEY® live on-campus events. YOUNG MONEY® is a leading authority for young adults, providing a positive, informative experience in a relaxed, youthful environment. www.youngmoney.com

MILITARY MONEY® Magazine, which explores the dynamic lifestyle of military families and serves as an authoritative financial resource for those serving in America's armed forces. Saving, investing and budgeting on a military income-while coping with frequent moves, career changes for the spouse, and new schools for the kids-requires special skills and planning. Created as part of the U.S. Department of Defense's "Financial Readiness Campaign," MILITARY MONEY® reaches an estimated 500,000 readers each quarter through distribution at military bases around the world and an engaging web site at www.militarymoney.com.

Interactive consumer credit and money management education software programs focused on specific aspects of personal finance such as goal setting, budgeting, credit basics, and credit reports. It is available in web-based and CD-ROM. ICEF Software is the recipient of the "Excellence in e-Learning Award," one of the e-learning industry's most celebrated honors.

InCharge® Radio. Save thousands on mortgage interest...get around dealer markups when buying a car...dig your way out of credit card debt! For listeners seeking to achieve a higher quality of life, Mike Schiano–voice of the Money Minute with Mike™–offers a fresh, friendly and easy to understand perspective on everyday family finance and is heard on more than 300 radio stations across the U.S. each day. A book author, speaker, and national financial columnist, Mike's unique blend of energy and seasoned professionalism make the Money Minute with Mike™ a popular program. ICEF's "Military Money Minute" segments are aired around the world on American Forces Radio Network. www.inchargeradio.com

PERSONAL FINANCE EDUCATIONAL PUBLICATIONS

These include the Mind Your Finances series of family finance booklets providing smart strategies for successful personal banking, spending, saving, car buying and more; *Next Step: A Monthly Guide to Reaching Your Financial Goals*; *Your Money: A Guide to Managing Your Credit and Debt*; *Mind Your Finances; InCharge® Guide to Homeownership*.

MindYourFinances.com is a web site developed and maintained by the Education Services department of the InCharge® Institute and offers a variety of programs designed to help people manage and save their money, use credit wisely, get out of debt and get motivated to gain their financial freedom. Inside MindYourFinances.com you'll discover extensive information on budgeting, managing cash flow, interpreting credit reports, using credit cards effectively, understanding bankruptcy and much more. www.mindyourfinances.com

Dinero Hispano fue creado para proveer educación financiera a la creciente comunidad hispana que necesita conocer la importancia de un buen manejo de sus finanzas para cumplir con sus sueños y metas trazadas. Dinero Hispano ofrece una variedad de programas diseñados para ayudar a la comunidad hispana sobre el uso adecuado del crédito y cómo tomar control de su situación financiera. Dinero Hispano ofrece información sobre presupuesto, manejo de efectivo, interpretación de reportes de crédito, manejo efectivo de tarjetas de crédito y bancarrota. www.dinerohispano.com

Learn more about InCharge® Education Foundation Inc. helpful resources by visiting **www.inchargefoundation.org.**

Your purchase of educational products helps support the foundation's mission and will help you reach your financial goals.

BrightScore™

Put your credit improvement program into fast forward!

When it comes to getting the best interest rates on credit cards, car loans, mortgages and more, there's one number lenders use—your credit score. And if yours is lower than it should be because of errors in your *credit report, identity fraud,* or *accounts past due* or *in collections,* you're paying more than you should!

BrightScore™ is an interactive credit report and scoring program that gives you **customized, comprehensive guidance**—and **personalized recommendations** to boost your score—all while providing access to live phone-based counseling. You'll understand exactly what's in your credit report—and how it's impacting your score. With BrightScore™, you get:

- An easy-to-understand credit report and letter-grade score
- A personalized credit analysis and action plan, with customized recommendations
- A tool to help find and resolve errors
- Access to trained live BrightScore™ counselors

Learn more about a BrightScore™ solution today—online at www.creditbooster.com or call toll-free: 1-888-801-0384.